MATT AND TOM OLDFIELD

ULTIMATE
FOOTBALL HEROES

SUPERSTARS
ROONEY · BECKHAM · GERRARD

FROM THE PLAYGROUND
TO THE PITCH

DINO

Published by Dino Books,
an imprint of Bonnier Books UK,
The Plaza,
535 Kings Road,
London SW10 0SZ

🔹 @dinobooks
🔹 @footieheroesbks
www.heroesfootball.com
www.bonnierbooks.co.uk

Rooney first published in 2015
Beckham first published in 2018
Gerrard first published in 2017
This collection published in 2020

Text © Matt and Tom Oldfield 2015, 2017, 2018

The right of Matt and Tom Oldfield to be identified as the authors
of this work has been asserted by them in accordance with the Copyright,
Designs and Patents Act 1988.

Design and typesetting by www.envydesign.co.uk

ISBN: 978 1 78946 332 3

British Library Cataloguing-in-Publication Data:
A catalogue record for this book is available from the British Library.

Printed and bound in Great Britain by Clays Ltd, Elcograf S.p.A.
1 3 5 7 9 10 8 6 4 2

Matt Oldfield is an accomplished writer and the editor-in-chief of football review site Of Pitch & Page. Tom Oldfield is a freelance sports writer and the author of biographies on Cristiano Ronaldo, Arsène Wenger and Rafael Nadal.

Cover illustration by Dan Leydon.
To learn more about Dan visit danleydon.com
To purchase his artwork visit etsy.com/shop/footynews
Or just follow him on Twitter @danleydon

ROONEY

TABLE OF CONTENTS

CHAPTER 1

OLD TRAFFORD'S NEW HERO

'Roo-ney! Roo-ney! Roo-ney!'

It was the sound of 75,000 fans chanting his name. Wayne just stared straight ahead down the tunnel. His heart was beating fast – in fact, it had been pounding since he put on the famous red Manchester United shirt in the dressing room ten minutes earlier. It was a long time since he had felt this nervous about playing football. But then this wasn't just any game.

It was 28 September 2004 and he was just minutes away from the start of his United career. Where was the referee? 'Come on, let's go,' he muttered to himself.

That night's game against Turkish giants Fenerbahce in the Champions League was the start of a new chapter for Wayne. He was following in the footsteps of George Best, Bobby Charlton, Eric Cantona, Bryan Robson and so many other United legends. Now Wayne would have the chance to add his name to that list.

As he thought about his whirlwind journey from the streets of Croxteth in Liverpool to the Theatre of Dreams, he smiled to himself. He had started his first Premier League game for Everton just two years ago and now he was about to make his debut for one of the biggest clubs in the world. The hairs on his neck stood on end.

A broken bone in his foot had delayed his debut and United had begun the new season without him. But all anyone wanted to know was when Wayne would be back. When would United fans get their first glimpse of the teenage sensation who had cost £30 million that summer? And how would he top his incredible performances at Euro 2004?

Wayne wanted to make up for lost time. His foot

had been fine in training this week and he just hoped that there would be no pain once he put it to the test in a real game.

As crowds of United fans walked down Sir Matt Busby Way that night, there was a different buzz in the air. Wayne would be making his debut and they were going to share in that experience. Many of them already had 'Rooney' on the back of their United shirts.

Just before the teams took to the pitch, Ryan Giggs walked up to Wayne and patted him on the back. Maybe he could sense the newcomer's nerves. 'Don't put too much pressure on yourself tonight. Just enjoy it – you only get to make your Manchester United debut once!'

He winked then shook Wayne's hand. 'The club's going to be in your hands some day soon. This is where it all begins for you.'

Finally, the waiting was over. Wayne took a deep breath and stretched his neck to one side and then the other. Showtime.

As he walked across the Old Trafford turf, the

Champions League anthem blared out and caught
Wayne by surprise. It was the first time he had
heard it for one of his games. It always gave him
goosebumps when he heard it on television but it
was a hundred times better in person. That's why I
had to make this move, he reminded himself.

He jumped up and down and did some final
stretches, and as he did so, he spotted his family in
the crowd among the sea of red shirts. His fiancée,
Colleen, was there with them. They were waving
and cheering. The last two months had been difficult
for the whole family and he was happy that they
were with him tonight as he put on the United shirt
for the first time.

Wayne's decision to leave his former club Everton
had shaken the blue half of the city. He had been
called Judas, a traitor and a greedy kid. Wayne would
always love Everton. They had believed in him and
given him a chance to shine. But he just had to take
this next step.

The Old Trafford crowd was so noisy, he didn't
realise that his manager, Sir Alex Ferguson, was on

the touchline and wanted a final word with him. Now aware of him, Wayne ran over. 'You were born to play on this stage, Wayne,' Ferguson said. 'Give these defenders the worst night of their lives. The fans want to see something special, so give them a show to remember.'

The football pitch was always where Wayne felt most at home. As he reached the centre circle for the kick-off with new strike partner Ruud van Nistelrooy, his nerves were replaced with excitement. After all, football had been part of his life from the very start.

CHAPTER 2

A SIGN OF THINGS TO COME

The Rooneys didn't believe in small parties. A real celebration meant inviting all the cousins, uncles, aunts, grandparents, friends, friends of friends and so on. And Wayne's first birthday in October 1986 was no different.

The planning had started months in advance – finding a date that everyone could make, sending out the invitations, choosing the decorations and the games, and picking the music.

The last item on the list was the birthday cake and Jeanette, Wayne's mother, rushed to pick it up at the local bakery on the morning of the party.

'Don't worry – it's all ready,' the bakery manager

said, seeing the door swing open and sensing her panic. He ducked below the counter and reappeared with a square white box. In dramatic style, he pulled back the lid to reveal a large blue cake. He looked at Jeanette for a sign of approval.

Jeanette smiled. 'It looks delicious,' she said. 'Perfect for an Everton fan.'

'Great – I'll just put "Happy Birthday, Wayne!" on the top and then it's all yours.'

Jeanette paused. 'Oh, actually, could you make it "Happy Birthday, *Little* Wayne!"'

The manager laughed. He was well aware that the Rooney tradition was to give the father's name to the first-born son. 'Good point. You don't want Big Wayne thinking it's for him!'

Jeanette made it home safely with the cake. The aunts and uncles were already there, blowing up balloons and hanging decorations from the curtain rails. The cousins were keeping Little Wayne entertained upstairs so that it would be a surprise – not that he really understood that today was his birthday anyway.

Jeanette saw lots of people in the house but her husband was nowhere to be found. She started to worry. He had been there when she left. Luckily, her sister had an update:

'Big Wayne just called. He'll be back in a minute. He's just picking up that secret present he can't keep quiet about.'

That's a relief, thought Jeanette. She checked her watch. She needed his help with a whole list of jobs before the rest of the guests arrived. And she was eager to find out what this mystery present was – all she knew was that her husband had spotted it recently with his friends.

Ten minutes later, Big Wayne rushed into the kitchen, out of breath. 'Okay, all sorted. Let's get this party started!'

Jeanette explained which jobs were still on her list and then headed upstairs to get Little Wayne dressed. She was pleased to find her son sitting on the floor playing quietly with a tennis ball. It was rare to see him so still rather than scrambling around. He didn't even complain when she changed him out of his pyjamas and into his outfit for the day. Some would have picked out a shirt and trousers for this special occasion, but not the Rooneys. Football would always be number one in this household and there was only one thing suitable for today – his tiny Everton kit.

Finally, the preparations were over and the party could begin. It seemed like the Rooneys had taken over the street for the day, with cars parked everywhere. Family and friends filled the lounge and kitchen, and everyone wanted a glimpse of the birthday boy.

The party was a huge success. The music, the games, the food – it was all exactly as Jeanette had planned. Little Wayne was on his best behaviour, charming everyone with his cheeky grin, complete with six little teeth.

As Jeanette handed out plates of birthday cake and bowls of jelly and ice cream, her mind was already turning towards the big clean-up after the guests had left.

But the party wasn't over yet. A big pile of presents sat unopened on the kitchen table – that was the advantage of having so many aunts, uncles and cousins. Jeanette was one of nine children; Big Wayne was one of eight. It looked like Little Wayne would need a new toy chest. She was glad that they had moved out of their flat and into this house earlier in the year.

Big Wayne couldn't wait any longer. He picked up a long, thin package with blue-and-white wrapping paper: the mystery gift.

'Time for presents!' he announced, with a big smile. 'He has to open this one first.'

Big Wayne dropped the package gently into his son's lap as everyone pulled their chairs forward to form a tight circle around the birthday boy. Little Wayne stared at the wrapping paper and then grabbed clumsily at the edges. Big Wayne crouched down next to his son and helped him undo the pieces of sellotape.

'This is so you'll never forget that you're a blue for life,' Big Wayne said, lifting the present so his son could see it.

It was an Everton sign, in the shape of a car

licence plate. Little Wayne was curious. He reached forward and ran his little fingers along the bumpy surface, perhaps recognising the club crest from all the Everton banners and decorations around the house. His next instinct was to put the sign in his mouth – but Big Wayne moved quickly to stop him.

'You don't want to eat that, little man. You'll crack your teeth!'

Little Wayne giggled.

Jeanette had been standing in the doorway, keeping one eye on Little Wayne as he opened the package and the other on her husband's proud reaction. Now she joined the crowd in the lounge. It had been an eventful year but with every milestone Jeanette felt so lucky. An illness as a child had left her fearing that she would never have children. But then Little Wayne came along.

She was stirred from her daydream by a friendly hand on her shoulder. 'So, he's an Everton fan, then?' her sister asked with a smile.

'As if there could be any other choice!' Jeanette replied, laughing.

One-by-one, the presents were passed forward. Father and son worked together to open each one – but Little Wayne's eyes rarely left his new Everton sign.

An hour later, the guests had gone and the house was quiet again. Little Wayne yawned loudly and rubbed his eyes. 'Bedtime for you – you've had a tiring day,' Big Wayne said, scooping his son out of his playpen and carrying him up the stairs.

He brought the sign with him. Once the birthday boy was in his cot and drifting off to sleep, Big Wayne propped the sign up on the window sill – out of reach but where his son could always see it.

CHAPTER 3

VACUUM TO THE RESCUE

At the Rooneys' three-bedroom house on Armill Road in Croxteth, Wayne got his own room. It made him feel very grown up. He had his own wardrobe, a little bookcase and a chest full of toys. He soon had two little brothers to play with as well – first Graeme and then John.

Even in his earliest years, things came easily for Wayne. He was good at every sport he tried, he showed natural ability at school and he had lots of friends.

But at night he felt lonely and scared. He didn't really understand why. Night after night, he would end up coming into his parents' bed. He couldn't sleep in his room. Sometimes he claimed there was a ghost; sometimes it was a monster under the bed or a werewolf hiding in the darkness. Even his Everton things – his lampshade, his duvet-cover and, of course, the sign on the window sill – couldn't calm his nerves.

'He tries to fall asleep, he really does,' Jeanette told her sister one morning. 'We've tried all kinds of things but it's as if his brain just won't switch off. Then we hear the little patter of footsteps and our bedroom door swings open.'

'Oh dear, poor little lad. Hopefully it's just a phase he's going through. We went through something similar with our little ones.'

'Let's hope it's that. We're trying not to panic too much. Plus, last night was better – Wayne kept the light on and had the television on quietly as well. That seemed to help him. But he'll need to get used to sleeping in the dark at some point.'

Remarkably, despite this lack of sleep, Wayne never felt tired during the day. Every morning he ran down the stairs full of energy, as if the sleepless nights never happened. He never used it as an excuse to miss school, and it never slowed him down during the lunchtime football games in the playground. He lived for those games, and he would sit in class counting down the minutes until the bell rang.

Then one afternoon, Wayne found an answer to his sleeping problem. Jeanette had decided that the house needed a good clean, from top to bottom, and a quiet weekend was the perfect opportunity. She and Big Wayne cleaned, polished and mopped all morning. Before long, the kitchen counters were sparkling and the floor was spotless. Time to clean upstairs, Jeanette decided.

She climbed the stairs and brought the vacuum cleaner with her, plugging it in on the landing. For once, Wayne wasn't out playing in the street with his mates. Instead, he was lying on his bed, bouncing a little football off the ceiling and humming to himself.

As Jeanette started hoovering the landing and the entrance to the bathroom, Wayne's eyes gradually felt heavier and heavier. The sound of the vacuum was soothing and he closed his eyes. Two minutes later, he was fast asleep. Jeanette smiled when she peeked into Wayne's bedroom and heard her son snoring.

Wayne didn't understand at first. He thought he had just fallen asleep because he was so tired. Why would he think it was anything else? When he took another long afternoon nap a week later while his dad was hoovering downstairs, Wayne realised that the vacuum was the secret to his deep sleep.

It quickly became part of his routine. After school, he would play football with his mates until it got dark. When it was time for bed, he would plug in the vacuum and drift off to sleep to the sound of his special lullaby. Hairdryers worked as well. Just any kind of background noise that whooshed or buzzed seemed to do the trick. Jeanette and Big Wayne didn't know what to think. They'd never heard of anything like this before. But they weren't complaining.

'Whatever works for you, Wayne,' Jeanette said. 'It's wonderful to see you sleeping more. But one of these days I want you to actually use the vacuum to clean up your room. That's what it's for, after all!'

Before long, the rest of the family had heard all about Wayne's new habit. His cousins thought it was very funny and they teased Wayne about it. Sometimes they would turn on a hairdryer and see if it made him sleepy. 'Don't fall asleep, Wayne,' they would say as they plugged it in.

The noise at night was a small price to pay for Wayne getting more sleep. It didn't seem to disturb Graeme or John, who shared the bedroom next to his. 'Thank goodness we gave Wayne his own room,' Jeanette said to her husband. 'Imagine if one of the other boys was trying to sleep in the room as well! We'll probably sleep better too if Wayne's not climbing into our bed in the middle of the night.'

Big Wayne smiled. 'That's true. I guess that vacuum keeps the ghosts and monsters away! But I'll be worried if we're still having this conversation when he's eighteen!'

CHAPTER 4

A BALL TO TREASURE

Wayne jumped out of bed when he heard the doorbell. He never wanted to miss a minute of Uncle Eugene's visits. When his uncle came to the house, it usually meant presents – and he always saved the best ones for Wayne.

'How's my little champ?' his uncle asked as Wayne flew down the stairs and leapt into his arms.

'Got any sweets?' Wayne asked, flashing a cheeky grin.

Uncle Eugene laughed. He searched his pockets and handed Wayne half a packet of Fruit Pastilles. 'Don't tell your mum!' he said, looking around to check the coast was clear. 'She'll blame me when you have to go to the dentist.'

Wayne's brothers, Graeme and John, raced into the room. The three boys were all in Everton pyjamas and looked more alike than ever. Like Wayne, his siblings didn't want to miss out on presents. They put on big smiles and huddled closer.

'Don't worry, I've got presents for all of you,' Uncle Eugene said, reaching into one of the bags that he had brought with him. 'I always take care of my favourite nephews.'

He handed small parcels to Graeme and John. As they ran to the kitchen to open them, they shrieked with excitement and kept bumping into each other. Then Uncle Eugene turned to Wayne, with a bigger bag in his hand. 'I've got something extra special for you. I know you love football so I thought it was about time that you had one of these. Every six-year-old should have one!'

Wayne grabbed the bag and glanced inside. His eyes were wide open in disbelief.

'A proper ball – a leather one!' he squealed,

running over for a hug. It was the new Mitre ball, just like the one the professionals played with. 'Thanks, Uncle Eugene. I've got to show my mates.' He turned to run away.

'Hang on, Wayne,' Uncle Eugene called. 'The ball comes with one condition – the first time you use it, it has to be at the park with me. I want to see it in action.'

'Sure. It's sunny outside. Can we go now?'

Uncle Eugene laughed at his nephew's enthusiasm. Wayne may have only just woken up and was still in his pyjamas, but he was always ready to play. 'Check with your mum. If she says yes, I'll take you there. I guess I'll have to be in goal, won't I?'

'You're always the goalkeeper. I need to work on my shooting.'

Jeanette said Wayne could go for an hour and he sprinted to the car. An hour was all that he needed. He loved the feeling of smashing the leather ball. He flicked the ball up and volleyed it, he curled it with the inside of his foot and then he jumped up for headers. Uncle Eugene was out of breath as he dived

28

around trying to save Wayne's shots. Usually, he had no chance.

Every time Uncle Eugene picked the ball out of the net and threw it back to Wayne, his nephew had a big grin on his face. The ball was a success.

'Wayne, when you're playing in the Premiership, just remember who got you your first football,' he joked.

That night, Wayne sneaked into the bathroom and washed the mud off his new ball. He wanted it to be shiny for the next day when he would be playing with his mates again. They were going to be really jealous when they saw it. None of them had an expensive one like his.

He dried the ball with a towel and brought it back into his bedroom. As he climbed into bed, he brought the ball with him and tucked it over the duvet next to him, cradling it with his arm. He didn't want to let it out of his sight.

But that ball didn't last long. Nor did the next one. Or the next one. Either Wayne was losing them in neighbours' gardens (one even ended up on the school roof), or he was ripping the leather and wearing them out from playing for hours and hours in the street.

'Not again, Wayne,' Jeanette would say each time, shaking her head. He always had a story about how it wasn't his fault that he had lost the ball. Sometimes he would try to blame it on Graeme or John. At least he was doing something active, she told herself, even if she often feared that a neighbour would call to complain about a broken window or a ruined flowerbed.

One afternoon, Wayne's grandmother heard crying through her kitchen window. Sure enough, it was Wayne. Pretending to be one of his Everton heroes, he had kicked the ball as hard as he could. To his dismay, it flew up and over the fence into the next garden.

Retrieving the ball seemed straightforward, to begin with. Wayne found enough footholds to climb up to the top of the fence and drop down into the garden. But climbing back over was impossible. Every time he tried to jump up, he slid back down. In the end, he gave up and cried out, 'Nan! Nan! I'm stuck. Help!' Tears rolled down his face as he sat on the ground.

His grandmother hurried outside. 'Wayne? What have I told you about playing out there? You can't just climb into other people's gardens. Stay there, I'll ask them to open the side gate.'

'Sorry, Nan,' Wayne said when she appeared. 'I was worried I would lose the ball. They didn't return the last one I kicked over and Mum told me to take better care of this one.'

'That's why you should take the ball to the park if you want to play outside. For a little lad, you kick the ball so hard. Honestly, I don't know what your parents are feeding you!'

But her anger never lasted long. She loved spending time with Wayne, and he knew how to charm his grandmother. An apology and a big smile usually did the trick and within minutes Wayne would be tucking into a bag of sweets.

CHAPTER 5

THE GEMS

The next summer, Wayne found a better option for playing football outside, and it was one where he couldn't get in trouble. The Gems Youth Club behind the Rooneys' house had a tarmac pitch.

Wayne discovered it when he was looking for a ball he had kicked over the back fence. As he tried to guess where it might have landed, he heard voices and the sound of a ball being kicked against a wall.

He pushed his way through some thick bushes and peered over a small fence. He caught a glimpse of a small football pitch with goalposts marked at each end. Three boys were standing in one corner playing with a ball. He knew them from the year above him at school.

Wayne walked round the path until he saw a little opening – just big enough for him to squeeze through. Suddenly, he was on the pitch.

One of the boys looked up.

'Can I play?' Wayne asked.

'Sure. We need another player. We're waiting for a couple of my mates to get here. We should have enough for four-a-side. I'm Joe. What's your name?'

'Wayne. I live just behind here. I've seen you playing at school. I go to St Swithin's as well but I'm in the year below. I'm only seven.'

'Are you any good?'

'I'm one of the best in my year. I've got a really hard shot.'

One of the boys laughed. 'We'll see about that.'

Soon, Joe's friends arrived and they were ready to play. They picked teams. Wayne was the last one to be picked. He couldn't believe it. He was usually picked first. He felt the anger growing inside him. The others would regret it.

Wayne played as well as he had ever played. Some of the boys were jogging, but Wayne was sprinting. Even though he was easily the smallest on the pitch, he wasn't afraid to knock the older boys off the ball.

Within five minutes, Wayne had scored two goals. But he wasn't finished. Joe chipped the ball forward and Wayne chased after it. He controlled it on his thigh and volleyed an unstoppable shot past the keeper into the top corner. He raised his arms. 'Hat-trick!'

Joe ran over. 'Nice one, Wayne. I guess I should have picked you first!'

Wayne smiled. He loved this pitch. He could work on his shooting, he could practise his passing and, best of all, it would be hard to lose the ball.

The game lasted almost an hour. Then the others went home. 'If you ever need another player, knock on my door. It's number twenty-eight,' he said to Joe as the other boys left.

But Wayne still wasn't ready to go home. When he found his lost ball under a neighbour's car, he returned to The Gems, this time alone. He had the whole pitch to himself. He kicked the ball against the wall and moved from side to side to control it as it bounced back. Then he moved further back and picked out a special mark on the wall. He took a run up and aimed his shot to hit the mark.

When he was tired of shooting, he practised his ball control. He flicked the ball up and used his feet, thighs, chest and head to keep the ball in the air, stopping it from hitting the ground. Wayne had seen the Everton players doing this during the warm-up when he went to games at Goodison Park.

In the end, he stayed until it got so dark that he couldn't see the ball clearly anymore.

After that, he was always at The Gems. When it was time for dinner, Jeanette would go to the bottom of the stairs and call Wayne to the table. If he wasn't in his room, she knew where to find him. She would go to the back door and shout his name. Five minutes later, Wayne would be back from The Gems, washing his hands and sitting down at the table.

'At least we always know where he is,' she said

to her husband one night. 'And it's safer than him playing in the street.'

Before long, Wayne was the one arranging the games at The Gems. He would go from door to door, asking if his mates were home and wanted to play. In the summer holidays, when school shut down for two months, there were eleven-a-side games every day. There was hardly room to move on the little pitch but that helped Wayne to create space for himself. He had to be quick on his feet to avoid being kicked in the ankles. Sometimes, girls from his school would come to watch the games, and Wayne always made sure that he put on a good show in front of them.

Wayne was rarely on the losing team – and that was just as well because he didn't take losing well. Whether it was throwing his boots or kicking the goalposts, Wayne's temper could be scary. His friends quickly understood how badly he wanted to win, even just in games at The Gems.

One afternoon, Big Wayne finished work early. When he got home, the house was empty. He decided to walk over to The Gems. Maybe Wayne knew where everyone was.

Big Wayne had seen his son playing football in the street before and he had taken Wayne to the park many times, but this was the first time he had watched him play at The Gems.

When he got there, he sat on a wooden bench. Wayne didn't see him, as he was focused on the game. The ball bounced off the wall and into Wayne's path. He turned and dribbled past one defender. As another of them ran over, he faked to go left, then darted right. With just the goalkeeper to beat, he didn't panic. He calmly curled the ball past the keeper. Big Wayne grinned. His son was the best player on the pitch.

When dinner time brought an end to the game, Wayne finally spotted his dad on the bench. How long had he been there, he wondered?

'Wayne, that was incredible,' his dad said. 'They couldn't get the ball off you.'

'They tried but I was too quick,' Wayne said, with a confident smile. 'But it wasn't a real game. We were just messing around.'

'Well, I think it's time you tested yourself in a real game for a real team with a real coach.'

Wayne hesitated. He wasn't sure if he was ready for that, but he loved playing football. 'Do you know a team that's looking for players?'

'A friend told me about a youth team run by our local pub. The team is called Copplehouse. I'm going to call the manager tonight.'

CHAPTER 6

CATCHING THE EYE

Big Nev, the Copplehouse Under-9s manager, blew his whistle and waved the boys towards him. The warm-up was over. Wayne scooped up his water bottle and jogged over with his teammates. He had been unsure about joining the team when his father suggested it, but now he loved it.

'Today's a big one, boys,' Big Nev explained. 'This team is above us in the table but we're just as good as them. Play your best and we'll beat them.'

As the referee blew his whistle and the boys walked away to take up their positions on the pitch, he added: 'Hang on, one more thing. I heard that scouts from Liverpool and Everton might be showing up today – so there's some extra motivation for you.'

Wayne's eyes lit up. People from Everton? At one of his games?

It didn't take long for him to make his mark. He won a tackle on the halfway line, raced past two defenders and fired a low shot from the edge of the penalty area. It flew into the bottom corner. There was no big celebration, just a smile and a clenched fist as his teammates ran over to congratulate him.

In the second half, he scored again. This time, he played a clever one-two on the edge of the box and slipped the ball through the goalkeeper's legs. The defenders looked like statues as Wayne ran rings round them. Sometimes it seemed as if the ball was attached to his foot.

As the game entered the final few minutes, Copplehouse clung to a 2-1 lead. Most of the parents were nervously counting down the seconds. But Big Wayne's attention was distracted by the sight of a white-haired man walking behind one of the goals, who seemed to be staring back at him.

Big Wayne moved nearer to the mysterious white-haired man, who slowed down and stopped. As the referee blew the final whistle, Big Wayne paused for a second to clap the Copplehouse players. Most of them were running over to Wayne, wanting to share the moment with the 'man of the match'.

'Are you Wayne's dad?' the old man asked.

'Yeah, that's me,' Big Wayne replied cautiously, turning around.

'He's quite a player – lovely touch, never stops running. I had to come over and talk to you. You see, I'm a scout for Liverpool and we'd love to bring him in for a trial.'

Forgetting for a moment that he had spent most of his life thinking of the Liverpool team as the enemy, Big Wayne felt excitement and pride.

'Nice to meet you,' he said, shaking the scout's hand. 'Wayne definitely picked the right game to score those goals. He's going to be over the moon.'

'Great. Here's my card.' The Liverpool scout handed over a business card and took a notepad from his back pocket. 'If you scribble your phone number down, I'll be in touch tomorrow.'

A minute later, the Liverpool scout was just leaving when Wayne raced over. Looking down at the red-faced nine-year-old, he said, 'We'll see you up at Melwood, Wayne. Great game today.' Then he marched off towards his car.

Confused, Wayne looked at his dad for answers. 'Who was that?'

'Who?' his father asked, pretending not to know what his son was talking about.

Wayne waved his arms impatiently. 'You know who. That man you were just talking to.'

'Are you ready to hear this? He's a scout at Liverpool. You caught his eye with those cracking goals and they want you to go and train there next week.'

'Liverpool?' Wayne asked, unsure of how to react. Usually his dad didn't like talking about Liverpool.

'This is a great opportunity, son. Try not to think about the rivalry with Everton.'

But when Wayne arrived at Liverpool's training

ground, something felt wrong. Maybe it was just nerves. Maybe it was some of the things he'd heard his family say about Liverpool. Or maybe it was the funny looks he was getting for showing up in his Everton kit.

Two of the Liverpool coaches stood together by one of the corner flags and watched him. 'He better be some player showing up in that kit,' one said to the other.

Even though he felt a bit uncomfortable, Wayne played well, and started to impress the coaches.

'I've been watching him – he's special,' one of the coaches confided to his colleague. 'His technique is excellent and he's too good for the other kids in the five-a-side games. Even if he's an Everton fan, we should bring him back next week for another look before making a decision.'

When Wayne got home, two of his older cousins were in the living room. They wanted to know all about the trial.

'I don't know how I feel,' Wayne said, collecting his thoughts. 'It was strange having a trial for

Liverpool. As an Everton fan, I felt guilty – like I was letting my team down. But Liverpool want me back for another session next week and then I'll find out if I got a place at their Centre of Excellence.'

CHAPTER 7

BECOMING
A BLUE

One telephone call changed everything. Wayne could only hear his dad's side of the conversation, but he sounded excited.

'Yes, he'd love that'... 'Well, he's got another trial there next week before they make an offer'... 'But this is the one he really wants'... 'Oh yes, that would be great'.

Finally, Wayne lost patience. He couldn't take the suspense anymore. Tapping at his dad's arm again and again, he mouthed, 'What? What?'

He eventually got his answer: Everton had also seen his game for Copplehouse, and they wanted him to come for a trial as well.

Wayne asked his dad to repeat the news three times before he believed it was true. He had been noticed by the team he loved – the team that he prayed would win every Saturday, the team that his dad had taken him to watch as a baby. He couldn't wait to tell his mates.

Later that week, Wayne and his father headed for Bellefield, Everton's training ground. Wayne was quiet on the way there. It all still felt like a dream. 'Good luck, son. Show Everton you're the star they've been waiting for.' Big Wayne ruffled his son's hair as he got out of the car.

Wayne felt right at home at Bellefield. The photos on the wall showed some of Everton's greatest moments, many of which he had seen in his dad's scrapbooks. Breathing the same air and walking on the same turf as his idols gave Wayne goosebumps.

On a quick introductory tour, he saw the cafeteria, the changing rooms and from one window, he could see the pitches, with freshly painted white lines. One coach was busy laying out cones while another pumped up the last couple of footballs and added them to a big pile. And all the special, distinctive smells were there – Deep Heat muscle spray, new leather footballs and freshly cut grass. Wayne never wanted to leave. Rain was falling steadily outside but he barely noticed.

It took about fifteen minutes for Everton to realise that they had hit the jackpot. And they weren't about to let Wayne slip through their fingers.

In theory, the other boys at the trial were his rivals but it was hard to think that way when so many of them were Everton fans like him. During the technique drills, he had an extra spring in his step – heading, passing, volley lay-offs. He almost broke the goalkeeper's hand with a volley in the shooting session.

When the five-a-side games started, Andy Windsor was the only coach overseeing Wayne's pitch. Before long, five coaches were huddled on the touchline, nudging each other excitedly.

'You'd think he was a few years older than the rest of the boys,' Andy said. 'They can't get near him.'

'I heard Liverpool are looking at him too, though,'

another coach replied. 'That would be a disaster. Imagine if we lost him to the enemy! We can't let him leave tonight without discussing Centre of Excellence forms.'

Ray Hall, Everton's Youth Development Officer, suddenly appeared behind the group of coaches. He had been watching from the other end of the pitch. 'We won't. I'm going to handle this one myself.'

Ray made sure the Rooneys understood that Everton was the best place for Wayne. He knew that they were big Everton fans and would probably need little persuasion, but this was not the time to take anything for granted. There was a potential superstar up for grabs.

'We treat the boys well at the Centre of Excellence,' he explained. 'The sessions are hard work but we try to keep it interesting. Wayne showed tonight that he would shine here. Think it over and let me know if you have any questions. We'll send a letter in the post and we can take it from there.'

The waiting was the hardest part for Wayne.

He rushed home from school every day to check the post. If the letter hadn't arrived, he feared that Everton had changed their mind about him or that another boy had caught their attention.

At last, an envelope arrived with the Everton crest on it.

'It's here!' Wayne shouted, opening the letter. He sprinted into the kitchen to show his parents. 'I got a place at Everton's Centre of Excellence for next season!'

Wayne had told all his friends and family the good news as soon as Ray Hall confirmed Everton's interest straight after the trial – but, without a letter of confirmation, some of them didn't believe him. Seeing the words in print made it feel real.

'This is huge, Wayne,' Uncle Eugene said excitedly when he heard the news. 'If you keep at it, you can make it. I mean it. Some kids have to make it to the Premier League level – why not you?'

'He's right,' Big Wayne added. 'One day some kids could have posters of you on their bedroom walls.'

Wayne giggled at that idea. But it made him think

about what that poster might look like. Maybe a goal celebration? Or a volley? Or a diving header? As long as he was wearing an Everton shirt, he didn't care.

His first season at Everton's Centre of Excellence confirmed that he belonged. Wayne worked hard in training – three nights a week – but he was always counting the minutes until Sunday morning because that meant real matches against other Under-10 Centre of Excellence teams. And he always saved his best for those matches.

Wayne made that Everton team unstoppable. He just couldn't stop scoring, starting with a hat-trick in his very first game. Big Wayne was keeping a running tally.

'Counting the nine goals against Preston, that's twenty-four goals in five games so far. Have you ever thought about going easy on some of these poor defenders?'

Wayne grinned and shook his head. 'Never.'

One of the games that Wayne had circled on the calendar was against Manchester United. Even though it was only the Under-10s, United were

known for their excellent youth academy and were
the team to beat in English football. Wayne expected
a tough game.

As he warmed up, Wayne felt the excitement
building. He didn't even feel cold, despite the chilly
wind. 'I want to make them jealous that I'm not part
of their Centre of Excellence,' he had told his dad
in the car on the way to the game. He looked across
the pitch and saw the United players passing the
ball back and forth in a circle. Most of them seemed
small and some of them were wearing gloves.
Wimps, he thought. No matter how cold it got,
Wayne would never wear gloves.

Everton's games usually followed a similar pattern.
Wayne would score a couple of early goals, the
opposition would lose hope and Everton would get
an easy win. That's exactly what happened against
United. Wayne's first goal was a tap-in. He preferred
the spectacular ones but they all counted. Two
minutes later, he fired a shot from the edge of the
box that flew past the goalkeeper and into the net.
He wasn't even sweating yet.

The United defenders tried their best to stop
Wayne but he was too strong and too quick. When
Everton built a big lead, Wayne liked to try some of
the things he had worked on in training – mainly
just to show off. A high cross gave him that chance
against United. A defender tried to head the ball
away but it looped up just behind Wayne as he ran
into the box. In an instant, he stopped, swivelled
and whipped an overhead kick over the hand of the
diving keeper and into the top corner.

Wayne ended up on the ground on his back
but before he could turn to see the ball in the net,
he heard a roar from the touchline. Coaches and
parents from both teams were clapping. John and
Graeme, who had made the trip with Big Wayne,
were jumping up and down and yelling. Wayne's
teammates dived on top of him and he was buried at
the bottom of the pile. He smiled as he jogged back
to the centre circle. He would never forget that goal.

After that, Wayne just kept scoring. In some
games it was six goals, in others it might be eight or
nine. By the end of the season, he had scored 114

goals in twenty-nine games. He was making it all look so easy.

'Son, that was an amazing season,' said Big Wayne. 'I hope you realise how special it was. Now, let's see if you can beat that next year!'

'If they offer me a place for next year, you mean,' Wayne said. 'The letters are supposed to arrive this week but mine hasn't come yet.'

'Trust me, you don't have to worry about that. You're a goal machine. They want you to be at Everton for a long time.'

But there was always a little doubt in the back of Wayne's mind – even as a nine-year-old, even after all the goals he had scored. Any time he saw a coach talking to his dad, he wondered if it was good or bad news. After most training sessions, he wondered if he had been one of the better players or if others were making faster progress.

His dad was proved right two days later when the letter of confirmation landed on the hallway carpet. Wayne opened it with shaking hands and then called his dad to share the news.

'Everton's letter just arrived. They want me back for next season. But it's even better than that. They want me in the Under-12s, not the Under-11s!'

CHAPTER 8

MASCOT MISCHIEF

Being part of the Centre of Excellence put Wayne in a good position to chase his dreams of playing for Everton. But it also brought other benefits. One of them was the chance to be a ball boy or even a mascot for an Everton game. Wayne had been a ball boy a couple of times and he loved being so close to his heroes.

Finally, a letter arrived with the news he'd been praying for. He was going to be a mascot – and not just for any game, but for the Merseyside derby against Liverpool at Anfield!

'Do you realise how lucky you are, Wayne?' Uncle Eugene said, grinning. 'A lot of kids would bite their arm off to be a mascot for the Merseyside derby. You better bring us good luck!'

Wayne couldn't wait for the big day to arrive. He started a countdown on a sheet of paper and crossed off the days one by one. He rehearsed what he would say to each player, especially Dave Watson, the team's captain, who would be walking onto the pitch next to him. Maybe the players had heard about all the goals Wayne was scoring for the Centre of Excellence teams.

But bad weather was about to ruin Wayne's plans. The night before the game, the rain had been keeping him awake, and when morning came, pouring rain was still lashing against his bedroom window. He looked out into the garden and saw puddles forming everywhere. At first, he wasn't worried. He had seen games played in the rain lots of times. Even his games didn't get cancelled because of bad weather.

The weather forecast remained grim, though. When Wayne and his parents left the house and drove to Anfield, the rain continued to be heavy.

The traffic was slower than usual, and there was even thunder and lightning on the way. When they reached the car park at the ground, Wayne spotted the sign for reception and raced out of the car. But he returned ten minutes later looking miserable.

Big Wayne rolled down the window, letting raindrops splash into the car. 'What's wrong?'

'The game is off,' Wayne said in a quiet, sad voice. 'I've been looking forward to this for weeks. It's not fair.'

He climbed into the back seat, slammed the door and burst into tears. He sat in silence all the way home and then ran up to his room.

Jeanette gave him space for a few minutes and then went to see him. Wayne buried his head in his mum's jumper and cried again. Jeanette wrapped her arms around him and stroked his back. 'Wayne, it's going to be OK. You'll see. These things happen. I know you're upset now but you will get another chance. You'll be a mascot for another game.'

Wayne felt better after that. His mum always knew the right things to say.

Fortunately, Wayne received another letter telling him when the postponed match would be played. He had to restart the countdown.

Time seemed to move so slowly. It felt like forever before the date of the game finally arrived. Wayne barely slept the night before. Not even the vacuum could help. He laid out his Everton kit on his chair and wondered what it would be like to walk out onto the pitch with the Everton players. He got dressed hours in advance and then paced his bedroom waiting for his parents to get home from the supermarket. He talked to himself in the mirror and worked on his handshake.

Wayne arrived at Anfield in a bubbly mood. Nothing could spoil this moment. Chris, the Liverpool representative, met him at the reception desk and gave him a quick tour on the way to a small room with refreshments: orange juice and biscuits. He would wait here until it was time to join the players in the tunnel.

Time stood still. 'How much longer?' he kept asking others in the room. He was soon joined by the Liverpool mascot – a skinny boy with blond hair. But Wayne stayed on the other side of the room. It was the Merseyside derby. He didn't want to make friends with a Liverpool fan.

Shortly after, a woman appeared with a trolley. It was the pre-match meal. Wayne had a plate of fish-and-chips and a can of Coke. 'I could get used to this!' he told Chris when he returned.

Finally, the mascots were called. Wayne was guided through two winding corridors and then through a side door into the tunnel. And, just like that, the players were lined up right in front of him. He felt his legs shaking. All the things he had planned to say just slipped from his mind.

He was introduced to Everton captain Dave Watson and they shook hands. Dave asked Wayne whether he was enjoying the youth team training and games. Wayne nodded but when he opened his mouth to speak, no words came out. 'Yeah, I love it,' he finally managed to say.

Wayne couldn't help but stare at the other players in the tunnel, who seemed bigger and stronger than on television. He felt tiny. Liverpool captain John Barnes was right next to him, within touching distance. Wayne tried to pay attention to every little detail so he could tell his family and his mates about it all. They would want to hear the whole story.

Suddenly, the referee gave a quick hand gesture and the players started moving down the tunnel. Dave Watson put a hand on Wayne's back and guided him out onto the pitch. Once there, everywhere he looked, Liverpool fans were cheering their team and booing the Everton players. It was the loudest noise Wayne had ever heard.

As the other players went through their final preparations, Wayne's job was to kick a few balls to Everton goalkeeper Neville Southall as part of his warm-up. It was part of the mascot experience. He had watched other mascots do it before – he knew how it worked. The idea was that Southall would roll the ball out slowly and Wayne would hit a shot back. But Wayne didn't want to just be like all of the others. He had something special and memorable up his sleeve.

When Southall threw the ball to him, he was expecting a few gentle shots. After knocking a few shots back, Wayne sensed it was time for his moment. He dipped his foot under the ball and chipped it over Southall's head and into the net. Some of the fans behind the goal saw it and gave him a big cheer. He beamed.

'Cheeky little brat,' Southall mumbled as he picked the ball out of the net.

Wayne was saved by the referee's whistle. He was called to the centre circle for the coin toss and a photo with the captains. This one is going on my wall, he thought to himself.

Everyone had seen Wayne's rebellious moment, and he worried that he might be in trouble, and that Southall might make a complaint about him. But back in the tunnel, everyone was just smiling. He was in the clear.

'You couldn't help yourself, could you?' Chris said. 'I have to admit, I've never seen anyone do that before.'

'I wanted to make it extra special. Now I can tell my mates I scored a goal at Anfield!'

'Southall didn't look happy. For a second, I thought he was going to chase after you.'

Wayne grinned. 'No chance. He wouldn't have caught me!'

He had a taste for it now. He promised himself that one day he would put on an Everton shirt for a Merseyside derby.

'Let's get going,' Chris said. 'I'll show you where you're sitting for the game. We've got matchday programmes for you too.'

'Great.'

'And try not to cause any trouble on the way,' he said, smiling at the boy.

CHAPTER 9

A FAMILY MOMENT
TO REMEMBER

'Boys, sit still!' Jeanette shouted. 'I won't tell you again. Graeme, let go of his arm and move nearer to Wayne.'

Today was a proud day for the whole Rooney family and Jeanette wanted a photo to mark the occasion. Wayne was still the star member of the Everton Centre of Excellence but, when his place was confirmed for the next season, no fewer than three envelopes landed on the Rooneys' doormat. Graeme and John had both been to trials at Everton. Now, like Wayne, they would also be part of its Centre of Excellence.

'I just want one photo, is that too much to ask?'

Jeanette pleaded. 'Show me the letters. John, yours is upside down.'

Wayne and Graeme giggled and tried to help their brother. 'Don't rip my letter!' John screamed. That just made Wayne and Graeme giggle even more.

Hearing all the noise, Big Wayne walked into the room to help his wife. He was still on cloud nine after hearing the news. Weekends would never be the same again, but he loved watching his sons play football. 'Stop messing around and listen to your mum,' he said firmly. 'You'll thank her one day when you've got this photo for your collection.'

The boys sat up straight and held up their letters, just as Jeanette had asked. All three were wearing their Everton kit. They looked like the happiest boys in the world. She smiled. It was a perfect photo. She would get it printed and framed for the wall. Maybe she could put it in the family Christmas card as well, she thought.

'I can't believe we're all going to be playing for Everton next season,' Wayne said excitedly. 'It's amazing! You're going to love it, I promise.'

'It's perfect,' Big Wayne added. 'Three Rooneys – one defender, one midfielder, one striker. Everton will be set for the future.'

'I'm the striker,' Wayne answered quickly.

'No, I am,' Graeme replied. 'I hate defending.'

'Want to bet on who will score the most goals?'

Graeme and John went quiet. They were both promising young players but neither wanted to bet against Wayne. Their brother could score ten goals in one game. People were already saying that Wayne would be the youngest player to ever play for the Everton first team. It wasn't easy to compete with that.

'Just make sure you play well,' Wayne added with a big smile. 'I don't want you to make me look bad.'

Big Wayne walked over and sat down next to his wife. 'Looks like we'll need to plan carefully for the weekends if we need to be in three places at once!'

Jeanette rolled her eyes. 'I guess we can forget about our plans for a weekend away together. Maybe next year.'

There had been initial excitement when the letters arrived, but Graeme and John became nervous when the first training sessions got nearer and nearer. Wayne usually loved to tease his brothers at every opportunity but he knew this was a time to be a supportive big brother.

'Wayne, what kind of exercises will they get me to do?' Graeme asked one afternoon. 'Will it be like the trial where we just played a game the whole time or is it different?'

'Usually it's a mixture of things. Some running, some technique drills – passing, heading, shooting – and then a few five-a-side games. But don't think too much about it yet. You'll be fine when you get there. They wouldn't have invited you if they didn't think you were a good player.'

Graeme beamed. Coming from Wayne, that meant a lot. He wouldn't say that kind of thing if he didn't mean it.

'The other thing is to remember to enjoy it,' added Wayne. 'Everything goes so fast that sometimes I forgot to enjoy every minute of it at the beginning. We're really lucky – think of how many of our mates would love to be training with Everton!'

'Yeah, my mates are really jealous,' replied Graeme. 'They all love Everton. Now I'll get to tell them stories about all the behind-the-scenes action!'

Once the season started, Wayne tried to keep track of how his brothers were doing. At family mealtimes, all the conversations were about the Centre of Excellence – who was doing well, where their games were at the weekend and so on. But Wayne's main focus was his own team and his own progress. He had even given up boxing to focus all his energy on football. Despite playing against older boys, he was the best player on the pitch in almost every game. He wasn't just scoring goals, he was setting up his teammates too.

On one occasion, late in the season, Wayne was leaving training after staying behind for extra shooting practice when he heard a familiar voice calling him. He turned around to see Ray Hall standing in the doorway, signalling for him to come over.

'I just wanted to tell you how impressed we all are with your hard work – not just in the games at the weekend but in training too. Keep it up. There is no limit to how good you can be if you stay focused.'

Wayne grinned. 'Thanks, Mr Hall. I'm going to do whatever it takes to make it to the top, I can promise you that.'

CHAPTER 10

ADAPTING IN DALLAS

'Where's Dallas?' Wayne asked suddenly at the breakfast table one morning.

'America,' Jeanette replied. 'Near the bottom, I think. Why do you ask?'

Wayne unfolded a sheet of paper from his pocket. 'I got this at training last night. There's a tournament in Dallas and Everton is sending a team. I'm part of the squad.'

Jeanette got up and read the rest of the sheet over Wayne's shoulder.

'Wow, that's a long way to go for a tournament. It says you'll be staying with a family in Dallas. That will be different. I bet it will be really hot in the summer.'

'It's going to be boring. I don't want to be away from my mates. What if this family doesn't like football?'

'I'm sure some of the other boys will be staying with families in the same area. Oh, did you read the last part, Wayne?'

Wayne looked. He rolled his eyes. It said he had to write a letter to this mystery family to tell them about himself. He sighed. He hated writing.

'What am I going to say?' he asked, looking at his parents for answers.

'You can tell them that you're thirteen years old and you play for Everton. And you can tell them why you like football so much.'

'And they'll want to know about your family and what kind of food you like,' Big Wayne added.

'You can't tell them you think they're boring, though!' Jeanette joked.

Wayne laughed. His mum was probably right about that.

Writing the letter wasn't as bad as he thought it would be. But it took him three attempts to write it neatly and with the words in a straight line.

When the time came to set off for America, Wayne was laughing and joking in the car on the way to the airport, but he went quiet once it was time to say goodbye to his family. 'I'm going to miss you,' he mumbled. He hugged his mum and dad and waved to his brothers. He could feel the tears coming but he was determined to be brave.

The flight to Dallas was the longest Wayne had ever taken. He was restless and the man in front of him kept tilting his seat. Wayne banged his knee into the back of it from time to time just to get some payback. There was no chance of falling asleep so he tried to watch some films to pass the time.

When the plane landed at the airport, Wayne was welcomed by the family he would be staying with. They had made a special banner so he would know who they were. Their house was beautiful and they gave Wayne a tour. His bedroom was big and he had a bathroom just across the corridor.

'We're really happy to have you staying with us, Wayne. Is there anything else you need?'

'I'd love a nap!' Wayne said with a smile. 'That flight was really tiring.'

Wayne slept for a couple of hours. When he woke up he felt really homesick. He missed his own room, his brothers, his parents and his mates. He missed being able to hop over the fence to The Gems.

When he sat down with the family for dinner, he wasn't hungry. He thought he might be sick if he tried to eat anything. But they served up huge portions and he didn't want to be rude. In the end, he just ate half of his plate of food. How am I going to last two weeks, he wondered?

But once the tournament started, he felt better. The Dallas family was so nice and he got along well with their two children, Jason and Susan. Jason was the same age as Wayne and he wanted to learn more about football – or 'soccer' as he kept calling it. At first, though, they had a hard time understanding Wayne's accent.

'Wayne, come outside,' Jason said after dinner one night. 'Let's play basketball.'

There was a basketball hoop in the driveway and

Jason disappeared into the garage and came back with a basketball that looked worn out from daily use. A bit like one of my footballs, Wayne thought to himself.

'Take a shot, Wayne,' Jason said, throwing him the ball.

Wayne had only played basketball a couple of times at school. He didn't know how to shoot. He just threw the ball towards the hoop but his shot missed completely. Jason laughed.

'Have another go. Shoot it with the fingertips and flick your wrist.'

Wayne took ten more shots. All of them missed and only one of them even hit the rim.

'Let me try something a bit different,' he said, taking ten steps backwards into the street. 'I bet I'll be better with my feet than my hands.'

He placed the basketball on the pavement and gave himself a little run up. Jason watched him in amazement.

Wayne chipped the basketball high into the air. He and Jason watched the ball loop up and then start to fall, as if in slow motion. The basketball swished through the hoop.

'Whoa!!!!!' Jason yelled. 'That was amazing!'

Wayne stood with his arms in the air. 'I told you! These feet are magical!'

Everton would do well at the tournament. Wayne scored two goals in the first game and another in the second game, and the team finished top of their group to qualify for the knockout round. But there was no perfect ending – they lost on penalties in the semi-final. The heat was hard to get used to and Wayne felt more out of breath than he ever did in England.

For Wayne, visiting Dallas had been a fun experience. He had learned a lot, tried new food and enjoyed the feel of American dollars in his hand. But when the plane landed back in England, he was glad to be home.

CHAPTER 11

AN INJURY NIGHTMARE

As Wayne settled back into his old routine and prepared for the new season, he hoped to land more team opportunities with the older age groups, maybe even with the Everton reserves. He loved the challenge of proving himself against bigger, stronger players. He was never afraid.

But in the first training session at the Centre of Excellence, Wayne felt a sharp pain in his right knee. He tried to keep running but every step made him bite his lip to stop himself from yelling. Two minutes later, he limped to the touchline.

'What happened, Wayne?' a concerned coach asked. 'I'm calling the physio.'

'No, don't bother. It's nothing. I must have twisted funny and I got a bit of pain in my knee. It's better now.'

But it wasn't really. He tried to hide it by keeping things simple and playing quick passes so he didn't have to run. After the next session, though, he felt the same pain in his left knee as well. He could hardly move, but he didn't want to admit it.

Joseph, one of the other boys in Wayne's group and one of his best friends on the team, knew something was wrong. Usually, Wayne was firing shots from every angle and racing all over the pitch, but lately it was as if he wasn't trying.

When Wayne went over to get a drink of water, Joseph noticed he was limping. 'Wayne, if you've got an injury, you should tell them about it. No one is going to blame you. Get the physio to take a look. You might be making it worse by pretending there's nothing wrong.'

Wayne shook his head. 'I'm fine. If I go to the physio, he'll tell me to rest it. I won't be able to play. I can't risk it. Plus, maybe it will fix itself.'

But the limping just got worse. Next, his back started hurting as well. It was time to be honest and work out what the problem was, so he told Big Wayne. 'Dad, I'm in agony. My knees are messed up and now my back is really painful as well. It's been like this for two weeks. What if it's serious? What if I can't play anymore?'

'Slow down, son. I didn't realise you had an injury. What did the physio say?'

'I haven't seen him yet.'

'Why not?'

'I was scared. I don't want to lose my place. I've worked so hard and I've got a chance to push for the Under-18s this season. A bad injury could ruin everything.'

'Knowledge is power, son. It might be nothing but you need to get it checked. You're still so young and your body is still developing. Trust me, an injury isn't going to change the way Everton think about you.'

Wayne looked at the ground and nodded.

One phone call later, Wayne had an appointment booked with the academy physio for the following day. He couldn't sleep that night – but not because of his knees or his back. He just kept imagining what could be wrong. Maybe he would need surgery. What would he do if the physio said his dream of playing for the Everton first team was over?

When he entered the physio's room, he was just desperate to get some answers. He lay down on the soft bench while the physio went through some gentle exercises to work out exactly where the pain was coming from. He moved the boy's knees in different directions and put pressure in specific places. Some of the exercises didn't hurt at all, but others made him flinch.

'Right, Wayne,' the physio said after ten minutes of tests. 'You can sit up. There's good news and less good news. Which do you want first?'

'The good news.'

'Okay, you'll be pleased to hear that there's no serious damage. In fact, this is something that a lot of youngsters go through during growth spurts, especially boys who play a lot of sport. It's called Osgood-Schlatter disease and it's the cause of all the pain you're feeling at the moment. I've had three other Centre of Excellence lads in here with the same thing this week.'

'What was the name?'

'Osgood-Schlatter. It's basically inflamed ligament and it's something we have to be careful with. You need to rest – that's the less good news. I know that will be hard for you but that's the only way to get rid of the pain. I'm afraid there's no magic cure for this. I'm recommending three weeks of rest and then I'll see how you're doing. If things are better, you can start training again.'

Wayne went quiet. It was a relief to know that it wasn't a serious injury but three weeks without football seemed like a disaster. He was used to playing football every morning, afternoon and evening. What was he going to do? Most of all, he hated the idea of missing Centre of Excellence games. He would have to watch from the touchline while someone else took his place.

The days dragged by slowly. After a month of rest, Wayne felt a lot better. He was nervous that the pain might return when he resumed training, but within minutes, he was charging after the ball, and his knees felt fine. By the end of the session, he had totally forgotten about the injury and he felt as sharp as he had before the pain in his knees started. He was back!

He made up for lost time in the weekend matches, scoring four hat-tricks and reclaiming his place as the team's star player. Still, the injury had taught him a valuable lesson: his dreams could be snatched away in an instant. Sport could be cruel like that.

'I've just got to make every minute count,' he told his mum one night as they watched television. 'Injuries are so unfair. I don't ever want to be watching from the touchline again.'

CHAPTER 12

MOYES'S MAGIC WORDS

Now sixteen years old, Wayne knew people were starting to talk about him as a future star of football. He was part of the Everton team which had reached the FA Youth Cup Final against Aston Villa. He had been hoping to play as well as he possibly could, especially as both legs of the final were being televised, but he felt frustrated as deep down, he knew that the opposition had been the better team.

With some help from his cousin, he had even prepared a T-shirt that he wore under his Everton shirt with the message 'Always a blue!' If he scored, he was going to lift up his shirt and show off the T-shirt for the cameras. 'The Everton fans will love it,' he had predicted proudly. But things had not gone to plan.

Sitting on the muddy pitch at an almost empty Villa Park, Wayne replayed some of the key moments in the game over and over in his head. Could he have done more? Would things have been different if he had taken his chances in the first half? With a bit more luck, he could have scored a hat-trick.

As he trudged back into the dressing room, he tried to stay positive. It had been a great run, even if the fairy-tale ending had slipped through his fingers. At least being named Player of the Final was a small consolation prize.

All around him, his teammates were as frustrated as he was. They threw off their shin pads and kicked their dirty kit into the middle of the floor. This Everton team wasn't used to losing – and now they would have to wait until next season to get revenge. It was going to be a long summer.

Suddenly, the conversations stopped and the dressing room went quiet. Wayne was hunched forward, removing the tape from his socks, and at first his view was blocked. He sat up and peered to his right.

Then it all made sense. David Moyes had walked in. He was standing near the door in an Everton tracksuit, with his hands in his pockets, talking to the youth coaches.

Moyes had taken over as Everton manager a couple of months earlier and Wayne had already met him once. Some of his teammates looked at the ground nervously but he felt confident enough to walk over and say hello.

'Hello Wayne – tough luck out there tonight,' Moyes said when the youngster appeared by his side. 'Don't forget how good your season was. We're very proud of what this group has achieved.'

Wayne gave a slight smile. 'Thanks. I've loved it this season. We just didn't want it to end like this.'

Moyes nodded and then gestured for Wayne to join him outside the dressing room to continue the conversation. Once in the hallway, he checked that no one could overhear them, and added: 'I've had some great reports about you. I've already watched

videos of a lot of your games and I've kept a close
eye on you since I got to Everton. I think it's time to
test yourself at the next level.'

'I'm ready!' Wayne interrupted, hoping he
sounded confident but not cocky.

'Good, because you'll be training with the first
team next season.'

Wayne's jaw dropped. He couldn't think of a single
word to say. It wasn't as if he had never thought such
a thing was possible. He had overheard his family
wondering aloud if it might happen and he knew
that some of the radio shows were calling for him
to get a chance in the first team. But it was still an
incredible feeling to hear it straight from the Everton
manager's mouth.

In an instant, he had almost forgotten about the
disappointment of losing the FA Youth Cup Final.

'Don't let it go to your head and keep it to yourself
for now,' Moyes told him. 'We just want to see how
you get on at that level. We can't move too fast.
You'll have to be patient.'

Wayne knew he could be patient. He could be

anything if it meant playing for the Everton first
team. He finished changing out of his kit and headed
for the showers. The hot water felt good after playing
on a rainy night.

As he put on his trousers and his Everton blazer,
he was still floating on air. He felt a bit dizzy. His
coach then gave a short speech which was greeted
with some half-hearted clapping, but Wayne
couldn't remember a single word of it. His mind was
elsewhere, dreaming about what lay ahead. Maybe
the nerves would come later but, for now, it was
just pure excitement. He did, however, feel a bit
guilty to be feeling so happy when the rest of his his
teammates all looked so miserable.

But it was only natural that he felt excited. It
meant that when the Premier League fixture list was
released, Everton's games would be *his* games. If he
proved himself, he might get to play at Old Trafford
and Anfield. It was going to be easy to motivate himself
over the summer. By the time that pre-season training
was due to begin in July, he would be raring to go.

Over and over again, he kept replaying David

Moyes's words. *You'll be training with the first team next season. You'll be training with the first team next season.*

For a second, he thought about keeping it a secret and announcing it when the whole family would be together. After all, his aunts, uncles and cousins had all played their part in encouraging him over the years. But once he saw his dad waiting outside the Villa Park ground in the car park, he knew he couldn't delay telling someone. Confident that the team bus wouldn't leave without him, he raced over to share the news with him.

After seeing Aston Villa lift the Cup Final trophy, Big Wayne was expecting his son to be quiet or angry or both. Instead, he had a grin plastered all over his face.

'Wayne, have you forgotten the final score?'

'Of course not, but I just got some news that trumps that. David Moyes came to see us after the game. He took me aside and told me I would be promoted to the first team next season. I'm going to be training with my heroes! Can you believe that?!'

Big Wayne's eyes lit up. He was speechless for a moment. Then he just pulled his son towards him and gave him a big bear hug. 'A Rooney playing for Everton! You deserve it, son. Wow, this is a day you'll never forget. I certainly won't forget it.'

The horn on the bus sounded and Wayne saw that they were all waiting for him. The driver was waving for him to hurry up. They had a long drive ahead and it was already late.

'Dad, I've got to go but I'll see you at home. I'll tell you about the rest of the conversation then. Thanks for coming down for the game. Sorry we didn't put on a better show.'

As Wayne walked away towards the bus, he wondered if he'd spotted a tear in his father's eye. 'I'm proud of you, son!' Big Wayne called out. Then he climbed into his car, turned the music up loud and started his drive home, smiling all the way.

CHAPTER 13

IN DREAMLAND WITH COLLEEN

Over the years, Wayne got to know all of the neighbours in his street. Most of the boys had played football together outside, or at The Gems – before school, after school and into the evening until it got too dark.

But there was one particular neighbour that Wayne did not get to see as often as he wanted – Colleen McLoughlin. She was one of the prettiest girls he had ever seen, and the McLoughlin and Rooney families knew each other well. In fact, Wayne's cousin Claire was one of her friends. The two families met up a few times a year for barbeques and birthday parties. The McLoughlins were Liverpool fans, but any rivalry was friendly.

Even though the families were friends, though, Colleen didn't speak to Wayne much. He wasn't sure why. Maybe it was because he had accidently broken her brother's tennis racket a few years ago. He had apologised and explained how it happened but she obviously hadn't forgotten it.

Colleen was never rude to Wayne, though; she just had different interests and she chose to spend her time with other girls. When he was playing football, she was usually at a dance practice or an acting lesson.

Unfortunately for Wayne, his progress through the ranks at Everton would not be enough to win her heart. He knew her brothers but she didn't usually hang around with them. And the few times that she did come and watch the football in the street, she didn't seem impressed by Wayne's attempts to show off.

It was going to take something special to attract her attention.

'Oh come on, get me a date with her,' he begged her brothers on a regular basis. 'She doesn't care about me playing for Everton. I don't know how else to impress her.'

They passed on the message. 'Tell Wayne he can call me if he wants to ask me out,' Colleen told her brothers. 'He shouldn't get you to do it for him.'

'Why don't you come and see him tomorrow night? We'll be playing footie again after school.'

'I can't. I have a dance class. But I've seen him in the streets, yelling and showing off. All he talks about is football. I don't like boys like that.'

A few weeks later, though, the perfect moment finally came about. Wayne was busy doing what he usually did on a week night – playing football in the street. Then two girls appeared on a bike. And one of them was Colleen.

With sweat pouring down his face, scuffed shoes and a bloody cut on his elbow, Wayne realised he didn't look his best. Not that he ever spent much time styling his hair or picking out fancy clothes. That just wasn't him.

'Hi, Colleen,' he called, pushing other boys aside to make sure she saw him.

Colleen waved back, but she was distracted by a problem with the bike. Something was wrong – Wayne thought maybe a tyre was flat or the brakes had given up. He was worried for her. Colleen pushed the bike on to the pavement and approached Wayne, who was with one of her brothers.

'Can you take a look at the bike? The chain keeps catching and we're afraid it's going to snap off. Dad will be furious if I've broken it already.'

Wayne knew this was his chance. 'I'll fix it,' he said, before anyone could either offer to help or point out that he was a disaster when it came to fixing anything.

Colleen's admirer looked closely at the chain. It was just as he thought – he had no idea what was wrong or how to fix it. But Colleen needed his help. She was depending on him.

'Don't worry. I'll hook it back on. Just give me two minutes.'

Ten minutes later, after trying everything else he

could think of, Wayne finally struck gold. The chain clicked back into place and the bike was good as new.

Colleen ran over and hugged Wayne, who went bright red.

'Want to go for a walk?' he mumbled.

Colleen thought about it. She owed him that at least. 'Sure, but I've got to be home for dance class by eight.'

For Wayne, training with Everton was great but spending time with Colleen was just as good, maybe even better. In some ways, they didn't have much in common. But conversation came easily and naturally. He couldn't stop staring at her. They talked about all kinds of things, and he was determined to show her that he wasn't just the loud boy who played football in the street.

'That's not how I am all the time. I'll prove it to you. I'm a bit cocky when I'm playing football, that's all.'

Colleen smiled. She was starting to appreciate Wayne's gentler side.

'You're saying all this but how do I know if I can believe you?' she asked, winking at him.

'Easy. Let me take you to see a film at the weekend. I'll be on my best behaviour. You can even pick the film.'

'I see what you're trying to do.' She laughed. 'I guess I'll have to go on a proper date with you to find out then.'

It was all going to plan. He would do anything to spend more time with Colleen. With every minute he spent with her, Wayne liked her more and more.

But now it was time to walk Colleen home, and he needed to make her aware of how much he liked her. When they passed behind a building, out of sight of the neighbours, he leaned in and kissed her. Colleen kissed him back. Wayne was in dreamland.

When they said goodnight, Wayne promised to call the next day to arrange their date at the weekend.

'I'm looking forward to it,' she said. 'Just don't wear your Everton kit!' She went inside and then waved to Wayne from the window.

Wayne skipped all the way home. His prayers had been answered. He had a chance with Colleen.

CHAPTER 14

FIRST STEPS IN THE FIRST TEAM

Wayne had been waiting all summer for pre-season training to start, but finally he was on the way to Bellefield, then Everton's training ground. Big Wayne insisted on driving him there – and Wayne suspected that his dad probably hoped to stick around and watch the sessions.

He was surprised that he didn't feel more nervous. But he really felt sure that he was good enough to train with the first team. He had watched a lot of Everton games last season and thought he could make a difference. Naturally, his family agreed.

'I reckon it'll take about a week for Moyes to see that you need to be starting,' Uncle Eugene said.

'Duncan Ferguson and Kevin Campbell are nearing the end of their careers. Both of them have been great for Everton but it's time to look to the future.'

Wayne's first stop on arriving at Bellefield was the reception counter. He had papers to fill out and he had to pick up his training kit. But as he was not yet even seventeen, or eligible for a driving licence, he wouldn't need a parking space.

He found out that he had been given the number 18 shirt for the 2002/03 season. It had been Paul Gascoigne's number last season so Wayne was stepping into big shoes. He was too young to have seen all of Gazza's career but he knew what a great player he was.

Manager David Moyes brought Wayne into the dressing room and did some introductions, even though the youngster recognised everyone in the squad and they had clearly all heard about him.

The Everton players were very welcoming. Well, most of them were. A few teased him about his clothes, but if they had expected Wayne to come into the squad and be shy or quiet, they thought wrong.

He was one of the loudest in the dressing room from day one.

Once training started, Wayne proved that he belonged. He came alive when the coaches set up a 'forwards-against-defenders' session. He got a few strong 'welcome to the first team' tackles from David Unsworth and David Weir. But he responded by nutmegging Unsworth and firing a shot into the bottom corner. He then muscled Weir off the ball and hit the post with a volley.

'Nice shot,' Mark Pembridge shouted. 'You play like a pitbull so we'll call you Dog from now on. Everyone has to have a nickname.' The nickname stuck.

Wayne played with a swagger but he worked hard too. By the end of the first training session, other players had spotted his remarkable potential.

'Nothing scares you, does it?' Unsworth asked him. 'I thought you'd start moaning after you got a few bruises. I can't believe you're only sixteen.'

'It's a good test for me,' Wayne replied. 'Defenders

on other teams are going to kick me even harder. I'm not scared but I need to be ready.'

'Well, if you have any trouble, we'll have your back.'

The highlight of Wayne's first day was talking to Duncan Ferguson, his childhood idol. Ferguson walked over to say hello but, for the first time since he arrived, the younger player was nervous.

'I can't believe I'm training with you,' Wayne said with a shaky voice. 'You've been my hero for years. You probably wouldn't remember but I wrote you letters a few years ago and you took a photo with me and my brothers.'

'Thanks for making me feel old,' Ferguson said with a smile. 'I still like to think I'm one of the youngsters. I'm excited to see you play. Anything you need around here, just let me know. Do you play computer games?'

'Yeah, I love them. I'll play anything really.'

'Alright. First away game of the season, come to my room. But be warned – I'm the club champion. None of the other lads can beat me.'

A few weeks later at Bellefield, Wayne stunned everyone into silence when he chipped Richard Wright from an impossible angle. To him, it was just normal to attempt a shot from there. But Moyes and his coaches just looked at each other. They didn't need to say the words; their faces said it all.

'Do you think he meant that?' Wright asked at the end of the session. Unsworth was standing nearby. He nodded. 'Knowing Wayne, he meant it.'

Later that season, Moyes would tell Wayne: 'Looking back, that's when I knew you were going to make it in the first team.'

As Uncle Eugene had predicted, Wayne had made the Everton first team more unpredictable, and Moyes wanted to test his young star in the team's pre-season friendlies. Wayne was unstoppable, scoring nine goals. But the message remained: be patient.

The day after a friendly against Athletic Bilbao, Moyes called Wayne into his office.

'Great performance last night, Wayne. You'll get plenty of opportunities this season. But you won't be starting every game. Your career is only just beginning and I want to protect you and give you the chance to rest.'

'But I don't need time to rest. I just want to play.'

'I know – and we love that about you. But this is a big change for you. The Premier League is so physical. You're only sixteen years old and you're still developing.'

Wayne nodded, but he disagreed. Everton need me to start every game, he thought to himself. He decided it wasn't worth making a fuss about it yet. He just needed to play so well that Moyes couldn't even think about leaving him on the bench.

He kept working hard in training and it paid off. By the time the 2002/03 Premier League season kicked off, he had earned his place in the starting line-up. One day after training, Moyes called him into his office to share the news.

'You'll be starting up front with Kevin Campbell against Tottenham at the weekend. We think you're ready for this. I'm not telling the media yet so that they don't put too much pressure on you. But I wanted you to know. The biggest thing to remember is to just play your game. Don't let them get under your skin.'

Wayne's fierce competitiveness was often an issue. When things weren't going well, he sometimes lunged into a tackle. That had to stop. 'I won't let you down,' he promised. 'I can handle the pressure.'

He tried calling his parents with the big news of his first team debut, but couldn't reach them. When he got home, Graeme and John were just coming back from school.

'Oh wow, I think that's the Everton star Wayne Rooney!' John joked, shouting loudly down the street.

'It is! It is! It's really him! Can we have an autograph?' Graeme joined in. Both brothers couldn't stop giggling.

'Good one!' Wayne said, smiling. His brothers would never let him get too cocky. 'I've got a bit of news for you actually. I'm starting against Tottenham this weekend!'

Graeme and John rushed over to hug their brother.

'That's amazing news,' John said. 'Have you told Mum and Dad? We need to get tickets.'

'You're the first to know.'

They liked that. 'Can we sell the story to the newspapers?'

'Actually, you can't tell anyone. It's a secret at the moment.'

As the family sat down for dinner, Jeanette and Big Wayne were still shaking with excitement after hearing their son's news. Wayne watched how proudly his dad behaved, as he wandered around talking to other family members on the phone. There was no chance of this staying a secret for long.

Big Wayne lifted his beer glass. The rest of the family lifted their glasses too. 'Wayne, Saturday is going to be a very proud day for this family. Congratulations. You really deserve it, and there's no pressure, of course. We only expect you to score two goals!' They all laughed.

On the Saturday, Wayne's alarm sounded at 7 am. But it was hardly necessary. He had been awake for hours. Everyone had told him to savour every moment in the build-up to his first start for Everton, but now he was too pumped up to sleep. In the end, he gave up and went to watch television downstairs. Before long, the early morning football preview shows started, and he poured himself a glass of orange juice as he listened to a panel of former players making predictions for the day's games, including *his* game.

When the panel talked about Everton's match against Tottenham, Wayne was the first topic under discussion. The panel urged Everton fans not to expect too much, too soon from Wayne. After all, they said, he was a sixteen-year-old youngster who was totally unproven in the Premier League.

'Not for long,' Wayne muttered to himself. 'People are going to know my name soon.'

His thoughts were soon interrupted as the rest of the Rooneys joined him in front of the TV, all sharing in the excitement.

'Today's the day!' Big Wayne called out, rushing up to his son and patting his shoulder.

'Just remember, if you miss a sitter, everyone will see it on *Match of the Day*,' Graeme joked.

'And if I score a hat-trick, they'll see that as well!' Wayne shot back, though he was trying to hide the nerves that were building inside him. He didn't have an appetite for breakfast, even though his mum was offering to make anything he wanted.

On the way to the stadium, Wayne was unusually quiet. His dad glanced in the car's rear-view mirror a couple of times to check his son was okay.

Wayne was just doing a lot of thinking – mainly about all the moments that had led up to this moment. He was a sixteen-year-old about to make his Premier League debut for his boyhood club. It didn't get much better than that. He was living the dream of boys all over the country. He tilted his head back against the headrest and tried to put the emotions aside.

By the time they reached Goodison Park, he was ready. Nervous, excited, curious – but above all, ready for the challenge. His heart was beating fast at the buzz around the stadium, the music on the loudspeakers and the excited faces of the Everton fans.

And when he walked into the dressing room and saw the famous blue shirt hung up at his spot with Rooney on the back and the number 18 below it, he could not wait to put it on and make his debut.

The pitch looked in perfect condition, and the crowd was steadily growing. During the warm-up, he soaked up the atmosphere. He felt lots of eyes watching his every touch of the ball – or maybe it was just his imagination.

After Moyes's final words, Wayne and the rest of the Everton team walked out of the dressing room and into the tunnel. He looked at the experienced professionals all around him. In the Tottenham line stood Teddy Sheringham and Jamie Redknapp. A few of the players were old enough to be his father. He tried to look calm as he stood near the back of the Everton line. Kevin Campbell was just behind him, cracking jokes and helping to lighten the mood. 'Good luck today, Wayne. If you get a chance, don't hesitate to shoot,' he added. 'Just smash it in the top corner like you do every day in training.'

The atmosphere was unbelievable. Even before kick-off, it was so loud. Once the game was underway, the home fans cheered every time he got the ball. Wayne didn't let anyone push him around. A few of the Tottenham defenders tried to wind him up. They said it was a man's game and there was no place for a boy. Wayne took no notice. He had expected some nastiness. He had a target on his back as 'the next big thing' and defenders would want to make a statement.

It wasn't long before the fans were on their feet – and Wayne was part of the reason. His pass set up Pembridge to give Everton the lead. Pembridge ran straight to Wayne as he celebrated. 'Great assist, Dog,' he said, hugging Wayne.

With the score at 1-1 in the second half, Moyes took Wayne off. Wayne didn't complain but he was confused about the decision. 'I didn't understand that,' he told teammate Alan Stubbs after the game. 'I felt fresh. I wanted to score the winner.' He was sure he was playing well enough, and he wasn't tired. He was getting some rough tackles from the Tottenham defenders but he felt calm, and he wasn't going to lose his temper. But he tried not to let his frustration show when talking to Stubbs in case he seemed like a bad teammate.

It was a disappointing end to Wayne's debut but he would never forget the feeling of starting his first game for Everton. He just hoped that he would get more opportunities to show his talent.

CHAPTER 15

BECOMING AN INSTANT HERO

Wayne knew that he had a big moment just around the corner. That's what he kept telling anyone who doubted that he would make it. Like David Moyes kept saying, he just had to be patient. But it wasn't easy.

That big moment came a few weeks later when Arsenal came to town. It was another full house at Goodison Park and the Rooney family had landed a stack of tickets. But, for most of the day, Wayne could not hide his disappointment: he was going to be a substitute.

'I deserve to be starting,' he complained to his parents. 'Being young isn't a good reason to leave me out. If I'm good enough, I should be playing every game. I don't need rest. I could play a game every day and he thinks I can't play two games in a week.'

Usually, it was Big Wayne who stepped in for the pep talks that put his son back on track. But this time Jeanette had heard enough.

'Are you just going to sit here and sulk?' she scolded. 'You're a Rooney – that's not how we do it. We fight. Get out there and prove he made a mistake leaving you on the bench. Complaining won't get you anywhere. Let your feet do the talking.'

She's got a point, Wayne thought. If he gives me a chance today, that's exactly what I'll do.

Arsenal had put together a thirty-game unbeaten league run and they were the favourites to win the title. Everton had nothing to lose. Wayne tried to stay calm on the bench but, as the minutes ticked by, and the score reached 1-1, his frustration grew. He felt restless. As a distraction, he tried to look for his family in the crowd. He was sure that he could make a difference. Maybe he would come on for the last thirty minutes.

But the clock ticked on. Thirty minutes to go. Twenty minutes to go. Finally, with barely ten minutes to go, he was called to replace Tomasz Radzinski. After a quick warm-up, he was part of the game at last.

'Get stuck in and don't be afraid to take them on,' Alan Stubbs told him, putting an arm on his shoulder. 'They're tired. You'll be sharper than them.'

Wayne felt alive and he was at the centre of the action, winning tackles and making runs. The crowd was suddenly interested again and roared, as if he had woken them from a nap.

Then came the moment that catapulted him into the spotlight. Thomas Gravesen lobbed the ball towards him and it dropped to him twenty-five yards out. Wayne didn't hesitate. He did what he had always done – he let his instincts take over. He turned, dribbled and saw that no Arsenal players were closing him down. He didn't need a second invitation, and so fired a booming shot towards the Arsenal goal.

His heart skipped a beat the second it left his

foot. 'I couldn't have hit it any sweeter,' he told his parents later. The shot rocketed over the head of goalkeeper David Seaman, off the underside of the crossbar, and into the roof of the net.

Wayne didn't have time to think about his goal celebration. Pure joy took over. The crowd erupted. Fans were screaming, jumping, hugging. Everyone on the Everton bench was on their feet. So was Ray Hall, who had moved so quickly to sign Wayne for the Centre of Excellence, and who was also at Goodison Park that afternoon. Wayne's teammates raced after him and jumped on his back. It was a blur – just blue everywhere.

With just one kick of the ball, all Wayne's anger and frustration had been replaced with euphoria and triumph. Up in the crowd, Jeanette sobbed with pride. At the final whistle, the Everton fans chanted 'Roo-ney!' at the tops of their voices.

After the final whistle, it was all about Wayne. Moyes hugged him and his teammates gave him high fives until his palms stung. Every question, every conversation, every story was about Wayne.

Arsene Wenger was quick to praise the young match-winner. It meant a lot to Wayne that the Arsenal manager called him the best English player he had seen since taking the job at Highbury back in 1996.

And Wayne's goal had set yet another record. He was the youngest ever Premier League goalscorer. He hadn't even turned seventeen yet.

After the game, Wayne went to the pub with his dad. The locals couldn't believe it when the match-winner walked through the door. 'Wayne, you're a star now,' the owner said. 'You won't be able to have a quiet drink ever again.' Everyone wanted a word with him, asking him to describe the goal for them and telling him that he was going to lead Everton to lots of trophies. When it was time to leave, he had to push his way through the crowds to reach the door.

By the time *Match of the Day* began that night, celebrations at the Rooneys' house were in full swing. As Wayne's wonder strike was replayed from every angle, each family member wanted to have the last word.

'What a hit!'

'That's a definite goal of the season contender.'

'Yeah, and look at the crossbar shake after Wayne's shot.'

Wayne sat quietly, only half listening to the conversation. He was emotionally and physically drained. Sure, he'd only played for ten minutes in that Arsenal game, but it was the most dramatic ten minutes of his life. It definitely hadn't sunk in yet, but he got the sense that life would never be the same again. When he woke up the next morning, it all felt like a dream.

CHAPTER 16

CHEWING HIS WAY INTO TROUBLE

Drops of sweat formed on Wayne's forehead. It was so hot. Didn't they have air conditioning in here?

He had been thrilled when he heard that he was nominated in the Young Sports Personality category at the BBC Sports Personality of the Year awards. It meant a trip to London, staying in a fancy hotel and getting to meet some of the top athletes in the world.

He called Colleen straightaway.

'How do you fancy a night in London next month?'

'What? Are you serious?'

'You bet. What do you think? The *Sports*

Personality of the Year show is in a couple of weeks and I'm up for an award.'

'Congratulations, babe. That's amazing. I'd love to go. Let me speak to Mum and Dad about it. I'll need to buy a new dress, of course!'

A romantic trip and the possibility of winning another award. This was going to be great, Wayne thought.

But Everton had other ideas. They told Wayne after a training session that Colleen could not go with him to the event. Wayne was furious and stormed home. He went for a long walk to calm down but it didn't really help.

'It was none of their business!' he shouted when his mum asked about it. 'It's not an Everton event. I can't believe this.'

'What was the reason?'

'Apparently, it would send the wrong message. Colleen had bought a dress and shoes. Now she'll have to return them. She's going to be crushed.'

Wayne considered not attending the event as a protest. But in the end he travelled down to London

and checked in at one of the most expensive hotels
he had ever seen. He was afraid to touch anything.
'I'm just glad that I won't be paying the bill,' he told
his mum.

When he arrived for the event, he saw famous
athletes everywhere he looked. Lennox Lewis and
Steve Redgrave were standing on one side of the
room. Paula Radcliffe was there too. He just wasn't
sure what to say to them. Would they even know
who he was? He went to get a drink and then took
his seat.

As he sat in the audience, Wayne was nervous
about all the cameras that were pointing at him. He
opened a pack of chewing gum to calm his nerves. At
least he'd have fresh breath, if one of the presenters
came over to interview him.

Finally, the winners were announced. The
nominations for the Young Sports Personality of the
Year award had been narrowed down to three –
shooter Charlotte Kerwood, gymnast Becky Owen
and Wayne. The fact that England's football manager
Sven-Goran Eriksson was presenting the trophy was

a big clue. He opened the envelope and called out Wayne's name.

Wayne gave a big smile for the cameras as he walked onto the stage. The trophy felt heavy. He delivered a short speech – he had prepared a lot more but with the cameras and lights and such a huge audience, he was shaking and just wanted to get off the stage without saying anything embarrassing.

As he returned to his seat, he realised he had forgotten about the gum he'd still been chewing. Maybe no one had noticed.

No such luck. As he got changed in his room afterwards, his phone rang.

'Wayne, what were you thinking chewing gum like that on national television?!' his mum asked.

'Mum, I forgot. Everything was a blur. Aren't you going to congratulate me on the award?'

Jeanette paused. 'Yes, of course, we're very proud of you. I'm just saying that chewing gum really didn't look good.'

Wayne hung up. He didn't want to talk about it.

The next day, to his disbelief, the gum-chewing became a national story.

He called Colleen. 'Have you seen the papers? Why is this such a big deal?'

'Ignore it, Wayne. They're just trying to sell papers. This is what happens when people decide you're a celebrity.'

'But they're making it sound like I don't know any better; like I have no manners. I heard someone saying I didn't do my tie up properly either. I'm still a kid – why do they expect me to be perfect?'

It just seemed so unfair. He wasn't used to speaking in front of big audiences or wearing a suit. It was normal to make mistakes.

'People can be cruel,' Colleen said. 'You won the trophy – focus on that.'

Wayne said nothing.

'You're going to need a bigger room to store all your trophies,' she joked, trying to change the subject.

It was all a learning experience for Wayne. He had been the golden boy for months but now he understood how quickly things could change.

CHAPTER 17

ENGLAND'S NEWEST SUPERSTAR

Wayne was proud to be English. He always had been. Playing for England, though? Well, he hadn't really thought that far ahead. He had dreamed of scoring crucial goals for England – like Michael Owen had done against Argentina and David Beckham against Greece – but he understood that he needed to make his mark at Everton first. As Moyes kept saying, he needed to be patient and remember that his whole career was ahead of him. There were no shortcuts.

Wayne was happy to take it step by step. If he could impress at Everton, he might get a call to join the Under-21s. And if he shone for the Under-21s, he might eventually get Sven-Goran Eriksson's

attention and join the senior team. Maybe that
would happen in time for the 2006 World Cup
in Germany.

One morning, Wayne was training with his
Everton teammates. He ran a couple of laps of the
pitch and went through a few stretches. While some
of his older colleagues seemed to need a long warm-
up to loosen up their bodies, he felt fresh from the
start. He could play a match every day of the week.

As he waited, Moyes wandered over to him and
handed him an orange bib ready for the first passing
drill. He grabbed Wayne's arm and guided him over
to the touchline.

'Is something wrong?' Wayne asked.

Moyes grinned. 'No, Wayne. Nothing to worry
about. Quite the opposite, actually. I just got a call.
You've been picked for England. Congratulations!'

A huge smile broke out across Wayne's face. He
was being noticed. This was the first step. He was
still just seventeen and now he was going to be in
the Under-21 squad.

'That's amazing. Who are we playing?'

Moyes looked puzzled, as if the question had caught him by surprise. 'I thought you'd know the answer to that. It's Australia at Upton Park.'

'What?! The senior team? I thought you meant the Under-21s!'

Wayne went silent for a second, still in shock. His legs turned to jelly. The senior squad? Really? He'd be sharing a dressing room with some of the biggest names in the Premier League?

He mumbled his way through the rest of the conversation, thanked Moyes and rejoined the training session with his head still spinning.

'What was that all about?' asked Mark Pembridge, who had been standing closest to Wayne and Moyes.

'I got called up by England for the Australia friendly,' Wayne replied. He couldn't say the words without smiling.

'Lads, Dog's in the England squad for Wednesday night.'

The other players gathered round and congratulated Wayne.

'Can you get your mum's permission to be out

that late on a school night?' Unsworth asked, jabbing Wayne playfully in the ribs.

'Yeah, maybe she can write you a note!'

'Wayne, just to make sure your ego doesn't get too big, go and set up the orange cones on the edge of the box,' assistant manager Alan Irvine said with a grin.

Wayne laughed it off. He was used to this kind of teasing by now. It kept his feet on the ground. He knew his teammates were happy for him. They even planned a special announcement at lunch in the cafeteria, where they presented him with a carton of milk.

'Well, you can't have champagne yet, Wayne!' Pembridge said with a big grin as he handed Wayne the milk.

After lunch, he called his parents.

'England's number 9! England's, England's number 9!' Big Wayne couldn't resist singing that chant when he heard the news. 'Not many youngsters are so good that they skip the Under-21s. Sven must have been impressed.'

'I didn't even know he was watching me, to be honest. I'd never seen him at Goodison.'

A week later, Wayne's Uncle Eugene drove him to the hotel in London where the rest of the England squad was staying. By then, he had overcome the shock. He still had butterflies in his stomach but he felt convinced that he belonged in the squad.

The journey by car with Uncle Eugene was tiring, but Wayne still managed to stay awake for the team lunch. It was hard not to be star struck when he walked into the restaurant and saw David Beckham, Steven Gerrard, Paul Scholes and all the other big names. These were the players that he had grown up watching. Luckily, he wasn't the only new boy and he already knew Franny Jeffers who had come through the Everton youth system.

'Welcome to the squad, Wayne. Call me Stevie.'

Wayne turned around to find Steven Gerrard standing next to him. They shook hands and swapped stories from growing up in Liverpool. It was a relief to break the ice. It was easy to forget that the other players were just normal lads like him who loved playing football.

After lunch, he was ready for a quick nap before the mid-afternoon team meeting. He wanted to be as fresh as possible for the training sessions. As soon as his head hit the luxury hotel pillows, he fell fast asleep.

The next thing he knew, there were people in his room – someone from the hotel reception and two members of the coaching staff. He glanced at the clock. He had overslept and was late for the meeting!

'What happened?' one of the coaches asked angrily. 'Get yourself downstairs. We're all waiting for you.'

Wayne felt terrible. He was embarrassed and now all eyes would be on him when he tried to sneak in quietly at the back of the room. It was the worst way to start his England career, but luckily, the other players didn't give him a hard time.

Sven-Goran Eriksson spoke to the squad and explained that everyone would get some time on the pitch in the game against Australia.

'No one is going to play the whole game,' he said. 'I want to take a look at the starting eleven in the first half and we'll bring out a different group for the second half. You'll all get a chance to play. Enjoy it!'

Things got better once training started. Wayne was eager to impress, hoping to get as much playing time as possible in the friendly. He stole the show in the shooting drills. Everything he hit ended up in the top corner. David Seaman was soon sick of the sight of Wayne!

'I'm going to have to retire if you keep smashing shots past me,' he said, fishing another ball out of the net and having flashbacks to Wayne's wonder goal.

'How does it compare to the Everton training?' Gerrard asked Wayne.

'Everything is a lot quicker,' he replied, after pausing for a minute to find the right words. 'I like how creative it is. I'll be suggesting a few things when I get back there.'

'I'm sure the coaches will be pleased to be told that they need to do things differently,' Gerrard joked.

The game against Australia was at Upton Park in
east London, home to West Ham United. As Wayne
sat down on the bench and heard the national
anthem, he felt proud. If all went to plan, he would
be making his England debut tonight!

But nothing went to plan for the home side in
the first half. Australia scored twice and it was left
to Wayne and some of the other newcomers to
rescue England after half-time. He was so pumped
up, he felt like he could run all day. As he stood in
the centre circle ready for the start of the second
half, he took a second to savour the moment – his
England debut. He hoped it was the start of a long
international career.

Wayne made an instant impact. His energy lifted
his teammates and he set up a goal for Jeffers. In
the end, England lost 3-1, but at least they had
pulled a goal back in the second half, and Wayne's
performance had been eye-catching.

In the dressing room, Wayne showed yet again
that he didn't lack confidence. He started joking with
the players who had started the game. 'Are you sure

that you're the first team? Maybe we should start the next game.'

Paul Scholes just stared at him.

'Wayne, come back when you've won a few Premier League titles,' Gary Neville told him. Wayne couldn't tell if he was smiling.

Since arriving in London at the team hotel, everything had gone so fast that he hadn't even realised that he was making history. At seventeen years and 111 days old, he was now the youngest-ever player for England. He loved setting new records.

Much to Wayne's surprise, Gerrard appeared holding the matchball, signed by all the players. 'Great game, Wayne. This is just the beginning for you. You're going to be a star for England for many years to come.'

Wayne certainly hoped so. He had loved every minute of his first England cap. And even after just a couple of days testing himself against the country's best footballers, he felt that he had become a better player.

CHAPTER 18

JOY AND PAIN AT EURO 2004

Wayne's Everton teammates talked about summer breaks spent on the beach relaxing ahead of next season. He liked the sound of it, but plans like those would have to wait during the summer of 2004. The Rooneys had previously huddled around the television to watch Euro '96 and Euro 2000, and now Wayne would be spending the summer in Portugal, leading the charge for England at Euro 2004.

The young player reflected on his extraordinary rise. In the space of a year, Wayne had gone from wondering if he would get a call up to the Under-21 team to being one of the first names on Sven-Goran Eriksson's team sheet. On the downside, he was playing well enough for Everton but still not as regularly as he wanted. He had scored eight goals in his first season and ten in his second, even though he was often coming on as a substitute. Overall, though, it had been a good year, especially as he and Colleen were now engaged.

As he packed his suitcase for Portugal, he wondered what it would be like to represent England at a major tournament. He still got goosebumps every time he put on the famous white shirt and playing at Euro 2004 would be the biggest moment of his career.

He knew tournaments could be long. England would have a few days between games and he would feel restless waiting in the hotels. So he packed lots of CDs and as many films as he could find in the house. Hopefully that would keep him busy. He crossed his fingers that there would be a hairdryer in the room in case he couldn't sleep.

'Missing anything, Wayne?' Jeanette asked as she passed her son's bedroom and saw his suitcase on the bed.

'Probably,' Wayne replied. 'You know I'm not good at organising my things.'

'Have you got enough underwear?'

'Mum, get out!' Wayne shouted, going red.

By the time he and his England teammates arrived in Portugal, they were desperate to get started. He lay down on his bed and started thinking about their first game against France. The French team had a lot of stars. He loved watching Zinedine Zidane and Thierry Henry. But they would be the enemy on Sunday.

There was a knock at the door. It was Steven Gerrard and Michael Owen.

'Want to grab a massage, Wayne? We're heading down there now,' Gerrard said.

Wayne considered it. It was better than just sitting in his room. 'Sure. Sounds like a good distraction.'

'Bored already?'

He shrugged. 'Yeah, kind of. What do you do with all the time between games?'

'You'll get used to it. The massages are good. We play cards a lot too – you can join us tonight if you want. We normally meet in Michael's room after dinner.'

'And sleeping is always pretty good,' Owen added. 'It's so hot during training – like it was in South Korea and Japan. I've always had afternoon naps at the big tournaments.'

Before going to bed that night, Wayne called his parents. He had promised to give them regular updates after his arrival, and he assumed that he wouldn't be paying the phone bill.

'So, what's it like being an England star at a big tournament?' Big Wayne teased. 'What's the hotel like? Are they treating you like royalty?'

It was good to hear his dad's voice. 'I'm bored,' he admitted. 'I can't wait for the games to start. But the other lads have been great. The team spirit is really good. We know we're not the favourites but we feel confident we can surprise people.'

'And you're the secret weapon, son,' Big Wayne added. 'These teams will know all about Beckham, Owen and Gerrard, but they haven't played against you.'

Finally, Wayne got his wish. He was told to be in the hotel lobby by 3 pm ready for the coach that would take the players to the Estádio da Luz, home of Benfica. During the warm-up and in the dressing room, he was louder company than ever, and was probably annoying the other players. He was so fired up that he had to calm himself down. As he picked up a bottle of water in the dressing room, Beckham put an arm on his shoulder.

'Keep a calm head out there. They know you're a threat so they'll try and wind you up. That was me in 1998 against Argentina. Don't fall for it. Don't even get involved in it. Just play your game.'

Wayne nodded. Ever since his first game for the Everton youth team, his temper had been an issue. He always wanted to win – and sometimes he wanted to win too badly. He would get frustrated and would go in for a wild lunge or shove a defender to the ground. Now, just minutes before his European Championships debut, he reminded himself that he couldn't lash out and he couldn't let his teammates down. The stakes were too high.

Wayne put on his headphones and listened to some of his favourite songs. He was starting to understand that the waiting was one of the hardest parts of playing in big games.

Sven-Goran Eriksson walked into the room and closed the door. He kept the message simple. 'If we control Zidane, we win the game. When we win possession, move it fast. Look for Wayne as the outlet. These defenders will be scared of him. Let's go!'

The players cheered, some exchanged high fives, others jumped to their feet and started pacing – they were ready.

As Wayne took his place in the tunnel, he didn't even look at the French players lined up next to him. He just shut out all distractions and pictured himself scoring the winning goal. He could hear the noise in the stadium – the players weren't even on the pitch yet, but the atmosphere felt electric.

It only took about five minutes for Wayne to realise that his manager was right. The French defenders *were* scared of him. He could see it in their eyes. He felt quicker and stronger. They were making desperate tackles to stop him and yelling at each other. He was even more fired up when Frank Lampard's header gave England the lead. In the second half, the French defenders looked exhausted but Wayne had plenty of energy left.

When he spotted a long ball over the top of the defence, he turned and raced after it. He was ahead of Mikael Silvestre as he burst into the box. This was it – this was the goal he had pictured in his head so many times. But then Silvestre lunged in and tripped Wayne to the ground. It was a penalty.

Wayne leapt to his feet and pounded his chest. He was happy to have won a penalty but angry that he didn't have a chance to shoot. The England fans roared. Among some of the world's biggest stars, an eighteen-year-old was dominating the game.

Owen came rushing over to congratulate him and others followed. 'Great stuff, Wayne. They can't handle you.'

But Beckham's penalty was saved by Fabien Barthez. Wayne couldn't believe it. If he hadn't been fouled, he was sure he would have taken his chance. With just under fifteen minutes to go, the ball went out of play. Wayne turned and hung his head. Now he was being substituted. He didn't feel tired but he had to come off.

As he bit his fingernails on the bench, he watched a nightmare taking place on the pitch. First, Zidane curled in a last minute free-kick to make it 1-1. Then in the final seconds Gerrard misjudged a back pass, Henry was fouled by David James and Zidane scored the penalty. Game over.

Wayne couldn't believe it. His body went numb. He thought he could have scored on the counter-attack. Now he would never know if he could have made the difference.

The England dressing room was as quiet as a library. Wayne just stared at the ground. It was the cruellest way to lose. Gerrard was especially quiet, sitting with his head in his hands. 'Chin up, Stevie,' Wayne said. 'We'll get it back against Switzerland.'

Sven let the players recover from the shock. Then he rallied them. 'The result hurts but the performance was excellent. We've got two more games and we control our destiny.'

If England won their next two games, they would qualify for the quarter-finals. France had been their toughest opponent and England had almost won – that was a positive sign.

When Wayne woke up the next morning, the loss of the game against France still stung. But when he got out on the pitch for a light training session, he was ready to move on.

Four days later, he played one of the best games of his career. With new-found confidence in the France game, he played with no fear in the second game against Switzerland. It took twenty-three minutes for him to write his name into the history books yet again – this time as the youngest scorer in European Championship history. Owen crossed the ball and Wayne powered a header into the net. It all seemed to happen in slow motion for him – the ball floating towards him, leaping to head it, and then the net rippling.

He checked that he wasn't offside and then raced over to the England fans, showing off with a cartwheel. Beckham was the first to jump on his back, and then Gerrard screamed, 'Get in, Wazza' in his ear. Wayne wished he could see his family and his mates back home, all jumping up and down in celebration. There would be quite some party in Croxteth tonight.

In the second half, Wayne was the star man again, thumping a low shot that cannoned off the post then the goalkeeper and into the net. There was no fancy celebration this time – he just jogged over to the England bench with a big grin, as if to say 'These major tournaments are pretty easy'.

Back at the hotel, his phone buzzed. It was his parents.

'Incredible game, son. How does it feel to be the most popular Englishman in the world?'

Wayne laughed. 'This was the best day of my life. We're back on track and nothing can stop us now.'

'Wayne, you should have seen it. The whole street was out celebrating tonight. Flags and banners and hats. We were being congratulated by people we didn't even know!'

The delighted player remembered the crazy excitement during the last World Cup. Back then, he was one of the lads out in the street dancing around. What a difference two years made!

'Hang on, Wayne,' Jeanette said. 'Colleen's here.'

Wayne heard muffled noises as his mother passed the phone to Colleen. 'Wayne, you're a national hero,' she said, laughing. 'You were amazing. I should be used to it by now but it's still so strange to be watching you on television. Anyway, I'm sure you've got some celebrating to do. I just wanted to hear your voice. I miss you!'

'I miss you too. I'll call again tomorrow, I promise.'

As the tournament continued, Wayne had more surprises up his sleeve. If football fans weren't paying attention yet, they soon were after he scored two more goals against Croatia. England were in the quarter-finals.

'You were unstoppable, Wayne. Terrific game.' Sven said, patting him on the back. The England manager had hoped Wayne would play well but never imagined he would be this good. He had been one of the best players at the tournament so far.

Back in the dressing room, Wayne turned the music up loud and started dancing. 'Quarter-finals, baby!' he yelled. At first, his teammates just laughed at him but soon they were joining in.

Sven was already thinking about the next game. 'If Wayne keeps this up, we can go all the way,' he said to one of his coaches.

Wayne had never felt more confident on a football pitch. And he was doing it against some of the best players in the world. Maybe he was just fearless. Maybe his legs were just fresher. Maybe he should be thanking Moyes for limiting his playing time.

The quarter-finals saw England face Portugal. The hosts. Wayne didn't care. He loved it when the crowd was against him and he could silence them with a goal or two.

Portugal had done their homework. They knew Wayne was the danger man. But all the attention on him meant Owen could shine. And Owen put England ahead early in the game.

Then disaster struck for Wayne and his Euro 2004 dreams crumbled. He challenged for a loose ball and a defender collided with his foot. At first, he thought he was fine. But then the pain kicked in. It was too strong. He was in agony. As soon as he dropped to the turf, he knew his tournament was over.

As he limped to the bench, tears filled his eyes. How could this be happening? Back home, the Rooneys sat in silence, heads in their hands. In an instant, Wayne's luck had turned against him.

Even sitting on the bench to watch the rest of the game became too much for him. As the pain got worse, he was rushed to hospital for an X-ray and then went back to the hotel to see the end of the match. To make matters worse, England lost on penalties. Just like that, his dream of carrying England to the final was all over.

For the second time in the tournament, Wayne was left to wonder what would have happened if he had been on the pitch. He couldn't stop thinking about it. He checked his phone and saw lots of messages wishing him a speedy recovery, including one from Colleen: 'Thinking about you. We'll get through this together. Can't wait to see you.'

As his teammates faced the fact that they were heading home, Wayne lay in his hotel room and stared at the ceiling. He couldn't face packing his suitcase. That could wait until tomorrow.

CHAPTER 19

TIME FOR A FRESH START

Always a blue? Wayne kept asking himself that question. He had believed it for years, thinking he would be an Everton player for life. He had written it on a T-shirt and he had grabbed the badge on his team shirt after scoring a goal.

But now he wasn't so sure. Even after returning from his heroics at Euro 2004 and being named in the Team of the Tournament, he was miserable. And he couldn't hide it.

'What's wrong, Wayne?' Jeanette asked her son, when she saw him lying on the sofa watching television for the third afternoon in a row.

'Nothing.'

Jeanette shook her head. 'No, Wayne. I know something's bothering you. You've been miserable all week. It's not like you. You're usually buzzing at the start of a new season. Is it just the injury that's getting you down?'

'I want to leave Everton.' He just blurted it out. He hadn't planned to; it just slipped out.

Jeanette stopped folding towels and looked at Wayne in disbelief.

'You don't mean that. Don't let your dad hear you say that.'

'I'm serious. I need a change.'

'Have you told Colleen? What does she think?'

'I haven't told her yet. We can work that part out.'

'It'll be a big change.'

'Maybe it won't be that far. There are big teams near here.'

'Please tell me you aren't thinking of Liverpool.'

'No way,' Wayne replied. 'That's the one club I could never sign for.'

Telling his dad was a scarier job. Big Wayne didn't say anything at first. He was in shock. 'Everton put you on the map,' he stumbled. 'They believed in you from day one. This is your home. The fans love you but they'll never let you forget it if you walk away now.'

'I can't face another season, Dad. I need a change. Newcastle are interested, maybe others too.'

'Now you believe everything you read in the papers?'

'No, but after my goals at Euro 2004, teams will be interested in signing me.'

Eventually, Big Wayne shrugged and let out a loud sigh. 'I can see I'm wasting my breath. Just do this for me – give yourself a few days to think it over. If you still want to leave by the end of the week then we'll speak to your agent and see what the options are.'

Wayne knew that his father had dreamed of watching him play for Everton for the next ten years or more. He could see the pain on Big Wayne's face and knew this was breaking his heart. 'Thanks for supporting me, Dad. I know it was the last thing you wanted to hear.'

Later that week, Wayne met with Everton manager David Moyes. It was a difficult, uncomfortable conversation. Wayne explained to Moyes that he wanted to leave and that he needed a new challenge. He wasn't going to change his mind.

As Wayne recapped the conversation for his parents that night, Big Wayne forced a sad smile. It was tough to take, but he would support his son no matter what, even if his time as a blue was running out. 'Let's call your agent.'

Things got harder and harder for Wayne. The Everton fans took the news of his departure badly. As Wayne watched the games while he recovered from his injury, he heard the fans chanting that he was greedy. He had become the villain.

Newcastle were still interested and Wayne started to imagine playing at St James's Park in the black-and-white shirts. It was a big stadium, with over 50,000 seats, and he had heard lots of good things about how passionate the fans were.

But thirty miles away from Everton at Old Trafford in Manchester, important conversations were taking place. Sir Alex Ferguson was pleading his case to his bosses:

'This is the future of the club. Wayne could be a Manchester United player for fifteen years. You all saw him at Euro 2004. He's a man-child and he's going to be the best player in the Premier League in the next few years. Put him in our team with Scholesy, Giggsy and Ruud and we'll be unstoppable. If we want the trophy back, we need to open the chequebook.'

'What if we wait until January?' one of Ferguson's bosses replied. 'We can speak to Everton again then and see whether we can negotiate a cheaper price.'

'We can't afford to wait that long. Wayne won't be available in January. He's too good. We have to act now or we'll regret it for years. Newcastle are already making a bid.'

The debate took six hours spread over two days. But eventually Ferguson got the answer he wanted. He had the green light to make a bid for Wayne.

As the end of the transfer window edged closer, Wayne was getting fed up with all the uncertainty. He just wanted to be playing football. His foot was feeling a lot better but not strong enough to think about playing matches yet. He wasn't even sure if Everton wanted him to play. The worst part was that it was now the final week of August, and if no one bought him by the end of the month, he would be stuck at Everton until January.

Finally, his phone buzzed. It was his agent, Paul Stretford.

'Wayne, are you sitting down?'

'Yeah, I'm just watching a film.'

'Well, pause it.' Paul sounded stressed.

Wayne reached for the remote control. 'What's going on? What are Everton saying now?'

'They got a call last night about completing a deal.'

'Have Newcastle officially made the offer?'

'Yes, they confirmed that.'

'Okay, great.' Wayne got up and walked into the kitchen to get a glass of water. 'It's a good club. Let's do it.'

'Hold on. I'm not done yet. That wasn't the latest news,' his agent said, excitement in his voice. 'Manchester United have just made an offer as well.'

That got Wayne's attention. 'United? Seriously?' He had a hundred questions. This was the call he had been dreaming about. 'Oh wow, we've got to make that happen. Champions League football and a chance to win trophies every season – that's where I want to go.'

'I thought you'd say that. How soon can you get to Manchester?'

Wayne laughed. Five minutes ago he was sulking and now he was talking about signing at Old Trafford. 'I'd walk all the way there if I had to. When would I sign the contract?'

'If the deal is done tonight, United want you there tomorrow afternoon.'

'No problem,' Wayne replied. He hung up and started making calls – his parents, Colleen, his cousins, his aunts and uncles. It had to be kept a secret, but Wayne was hours away from joining one of the biggest clubs in the world.

CHAPTER 20

A DREAM DEBUT

Recovering from his broken foot had been exhausting and lonely for Wayne. All he could do was spend early mornings in the gym, eat healthily to stay fit and watch games from the crowd as the new season began.

But it gave him plenty of time to dream about his United debut. He wanted to prove that Sir Alex Ferguson was right to spend big money to bring him to Old Trafford.

Some had said it would take time for him to return to his Euro 2004 form, but Wayne was fired up. 'They don't know me. If they did, they'd know I'm going to be even better.'

On 28 September 2004, he played his first game

for Manchester United against the Turkish team Fenerbahce. What did he have up his sleeve? How about a hat-trick? It took only seventeen minutes for him to score his first United goal. There was a real release of emotion – a combination of the joy of scoring on his debut and the relief of being back to doing what he loved most. The injury had been heartbreaking but he was making up for lost time. The big price tag might have been stressful for some players but Wayne hadn't ever really worried about that. He just knew he would score bags of goals for United.

He wasn't satisfied with just one goal on his debut, though. Later in that first half, Ryan Giggs fed the ball to him outside the box and Wayne drilled a low shot into the bottom corner.

His confidence was sky high. When United won a free-kick thirty yards out, Giggs prepared to take it. But Wayne had other ideas. 'Let me have it. I want my hat-trick.'

Giggs smiled. He admired the youngster's confidence. Ever since he'd walked into the United dressing room, he'd acted like he belonged.

Wayne lined it up, looked at the wall and curled a perfect free-kick past the Fenerbahce goalkeeper. Old Trafford erupted. He couldn't stop grinning. His performance had outdone even his wildest dreams.

After the game, all the talk was about Wayne's hat-trick. Was it the best United debut ever? Was he the best player in the Premier League? He celebrated the moment but reminded himself it was just one game.

Sir Alex Ferguson came over and shook Wayne's hand. 'That was some way to introduce yourself to the United fans! Terrific performance. We're going for all the trophies this season and you'll be a big part of that.'

'Bring it on!' Wayne said. 'I just want to win. I want to become a better player as well, but most of all I want to be a champion.'

'Well, you picked the right club, then.'

Wayne smiled. It had been quite a night and he was looking forward to meeting up with his family. But most of all, he couldn't wait for everything that lay ahead for him in a United shirt.

'Welcome aboard, Wayne,' Ferguson said with a big smile. 'It's going to be a heck of a ride.'

Manchester United

🏆 Premier League: 2006–07, 2007–08, 2008–09, 2010–11, 2012–13

🏆 League Cup: 2005–06, 2009–10

🏆 FA Community Shield: 2007, 2010, 2011

🏆 UEFA Champions League: 2007–08

🏆 FIFA Club World Cup: 2008

Individual

🏆 PFA Players' Player of the Year: 2009–10

🏆 PFA Young Player of the Year: 2004–05, 2005–06

🏆 PFA Fans' Player of the Year: 2005–06, 2009–10

🏆 PFA Premier League Team of the Year: 2005–06, 2009–10, 2011–12

🏆 Football Writers' Player of the Year: 2009–10

🏆 Sir Matt Busby Player of the Year: 2005–06, 2009–10

🏆 BBC Young Sports Personality of the Year: 2002

🏆 FIFPro World Young Player of the Year: 2004–05

🏆 Barclays Premier League Player of the Year: 2009–10

🏆 England Player of the Year: 2008, 2009, 2014

🏆 FIFA/FIFPro World XI: 2011

ROONEY

10 **THE FACTS**

NAME:
Wayne Mark Rooney

DATE OF BIRTH:
24 October 1985

AGE: 34

PLACE OF BIRTH:
Croxteth, Liverpool

NATIONALITY: England

BEST FRIEND: Darren Fletcher

CURRENT CLUB: Manchester United

POSITION: CAM

THE STATS

Height (cm):	176
Club appearances:	732
Club goals:	306
Club trophies:	16
International appearances:	120
International goals:	53
International trophies:	0
Ballon d'Ors:	0

★ ★ ★ **HERO RATING: 85** ★ ★ ★

GREATEST MOMENTS

 **19 OCTOBER 2002,
EVERTON 2-1 ARSENAL**

This was the wondergoal that turned Wayne into
a superstar. Two months after his Everton debut,
Wayne came on as a late substitute. With the score at
1-1, he controlled a long ball, turned and hit a long-
range screamer into the top corner. Wayne was still
sixteen and he had just become the Premier League's
youngest ever scorer.

23 MARCH 2003,
ARSENAL 2-1 EVERTON

Wayne quickly proved that his wondergoal wasn't a fluke. He dribbled at Arsenal's scared defence again and then placed his shot perfectly into the bottom corner. Everton lost this match but Wayne was making a real name for himself.

17 JUNE 2004,
ENGLAND 3-0 SWITZERLAND

Wayne was a surprise pick for England's Euro 2004 squad. He was still only eighteen! After a good first performance against France, he was the hero against Switzerland. Wayne gave England the lead with a header and in the second-half, he scored again to make it 2-0. There was no stopping the teenager.

21 JUNE 2004,
CROATIA 2-4 ENGLAND

4 days later, Wayne did it again. Croatia took the lead but two more goals from Wayne helped England to qualify for the quarter-finals. The first was a powerful long-range strike and the second was a calm finish following Michael Owen's through-ball. Unfortunately, Wayne hurt his ankle against Portugal and his breakthrough tournament was over.

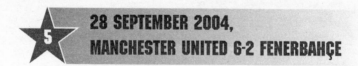

28 SEPTEMBER 2004,
MANCHESTER UNITED 6-2 FENERBAHÇE

Debuts don't get any better than this. It was Wayne's first match for Manchester United and his first match in the Champions League too. Was he nervous? If he was, he didn't show it! Wayne scored an incredible hat-trick, including a great free-kick. A Manchester United legend was born.

PLAY LIKE YOUR HEROES

THE WAYNE ROONEY VOLLEY

STEP 1: As the defender heads the ball clear, sprint forward to meet it.

STEP 2: There's no need to wait for it to bounce. Hit it first time!

STEP 3: Watch the ball carefully as it drops towards your foot. Stay cool.

STEP 4: Keep your head still and keep it over the ball as you strike it.

STEP 5: Kick the middle of the ball with your instep. That's how you get the best speed and power.

STEP 6: Make sure your shooting leg follows through in a straight line to keep your volley on target.

STEP 7: Don't hold back with your celebration. You've just scored a wondergoal!

TEST YOUR KNOWLEDGE

QUESTIONS

1. What did Wayne Senior give Wayne Junior for his first birthday?

2. What did Wayne use to help him get to sleep when he was young?

3. What did Uncle Eugene give Wayne for this sixth birthday?

4. Wayne had a trial at Everton's local rivals Liverpool – true or false?

5. Who was the Everton captain when Wayne was the club mascot against Liverpool?

6. When he was 13, Wayne travelled to which American city to play in a tournament?

7. Which Everton manager gave Wayne his first-team debut?

8. Who wore the Everton Number 18 shirt before Wayne?

9. Who was Wayne's England manager at Euro 2004?

10. How much did Manchester United pay to sign Wayne from Everton?

11. Which other Premier League club did Wayne nearly sign for instead?

Answers below. . . No cheating!

1. An Everton sign, in the shape of a car licence plate. 2. The noise of a vacuum cleaner. 3. A proper leather football. 4. True – but Wayne wore an Everton shirt at the trial 5. Dave Watson. 6. Dallas. 7. David Moyes. 8. Paul 'Gazza' Gascoigne. 9. Sven-Goran Eriksson. 10. £30 million. 11. Newcastle United

BECKHAM

TABLE OF CONTENTS

CHAPTER 1

ALWAYS A WINNER

18 May 2013 – Paris, France

This was it. After twenty amazing years, David's life as a professional footballer was about to end. He had always known that his final match would be emotional, but he was holding back the tears before the game had even kicked off.

'Am I doing the right thing?' David asked himself.

He was thirty-eight years old now and his tired body was telling him to stop. His head, however, was telling him to keep doing what he loved, and so were the PSG fans in the Parc des Princes stadium.

'Beckham, one more year please!' one of their banners read.

But no, he wanted to quit while he was still at the

top of his game, while he could still help his team.

During his career, David had played with so many superstars. He listed them in his head:

Eric Cantona, Ryan Giggs and Paul Scholes –

at Manchester United

Michael Owen, Steven Gerrard and Wayne

Rooney – with England

Ronaldo, Roberto Carlos, Zinedine Zidane

and Luís Figo – at Real Madrid

Landon Donovan and Robbie Keane –

at LA Galaxy

Paolo Maldini, Ronaldinho and Kaká –

at AC Milan

...and now Zlatan Ibrahimović at PSG. What a list! It was a great honour to be able to call them friends, as well as teammates. They had all inspired David to keep striving for improvement and perfection. Like them, he was always a winner.

'Are you ready, Becks?' Zlatan said, giving him a high-five.

'Ready as I'll ever be,' David smiled back, fixing the armband on his sleeve. The PSG manager, Carlo

Ancelotti, had made him the captain for the final home match of the season against Brest.

David's family was there watching in the Parc des Princes stadium, and the names of his children – Brooklyn, Romeo, Cruz and Harper – were stitched into his special white, red and blue Adidas boots. His children meant so much to him, and so did his wife, Victoria.

Next to their names were his shirt numbers – 7 for Manchester United and England, 23 for Real Madrid and LA Galaxy, and 32 for AC Milan and PSG.

And next to his shirt numbers was the Union Jack flag. No matter where David played – Spain, America, Italy or France – he was always proud to be English.

'Right, let's do this!' David shouted to his teammates.

PSG were 1–0 up after four minutes thanks to another Zlatan goal. It was party time for the Champions of France but what could David do to celebrate his big day? Could his remarkable right foot create one last bit of magic?

Ever since he was a young boy, David had worked so hard to make the most of his talent. He had an unusual technique for striking the ball, but hours of practice made perfect. When it came to long-range shots, long-range passes, free kicks and corners, he was the best in the business.

After thirty minutes, PSG won a corner. As David walked over to take it, he slowed down to enjoy the feeling of being so close to the fans. No matter what team he played for, the fans' noise and passion always left him buzzing. It had inspired him so many times over the years. David remembered his two late corners in the 1999 Champions League final, when Manchester United fought back to complete the Treble. What a night!

Football was never over until the final whistle blew – that's what his old Manchester United manager Sir Alex Ferguson had taught him. David chipped a teasing cross towards the penalty spot. It was another dangerous delivery, but could someone get on the end of it? His midfield partner Blaise Matuidi could. He hit it on the volley and scored. 2–0!

'Thanks, you're the best teammate ever!' he screamed.

David was pleased to get one last assist, but could he get one last goal? He hadn't yet scored for PSG but there was still time to say goodbye in style.

When his team won a free kick, the fans urged him to take it. But David was a team player, not a greedy player. It was Zlatan's turn to strike it. 'Just do me proud!' David told him.

'Yes, captain.' The Swedish striker bent the ball around the wall and into the top corner. 3–0!

'Beckham, eat your heart out!' Zlatan laughed as they celebrated together.

With ten minutes to go, it was finally time for David to leave the field for good. He had given his all, just like always. He took a deep breath and tried not to cry, but it was no use. As his teammates came over to hug him one by one, tears filled his eyes. By the time he reached his manager Ancelotti on the touchline, the tears were streaming down his face.

'It's a historic moment,' a voice boomed around the stadium. 'DAVID...'

'BECKHAM!' the fans roared.

'*Merci*, David!' they chanted.

David Beckham! David Beckham! David Beckham!

After the match, David walked around the pitch, clapping to the crowd. He had only been at PSG for five months, but it really felt like home. His teammates threw him high into the air, once, twice and a third time for luck.

'We'll miss you, Becks!' they shouted.

David was going to miss them too. He was going to miss playing football so much. Ever since his first kick, football had been his focus, his life. It was hard to believe that his incredible playing career was over. His adventure had taken him from London to Paris, via Manchester, Madrid, Los Angeles, Milan and so many other exciting places.

Through hard work and dedication, he had risen through the ranks at his beloved Manchester United to become one of the most famous footballers on the planet. Although his cabinet was already full to the brim, David had one last trophy to collect – the Ligue 1 title.

'I want to say thank you to everybody in Paris - to my teammates, to the staff, to the fans,' he spoke into the microphone, wearing an England flag like a cape. 'It's been very special to finish my career here. I feel I've achieved everything I could. I wanted to go out as a champion and I have.'

At club level, David had won the league in four different countries – England, Spain, the USA, and now France. He was the only Englishman to ever achieve that and he had also won the Champions League and the FA Cup.

At international level, David hadn't won any trophies but there was still so much to be proud of. He had won 115 caps for his country, 58 as captain. He had played at three World Cups, scoring in each of them.

No, he hadn't quite managed to lead the Three Lions to glory, but David had bounced back from national villain in 1998 to become a national hero again in 2001, thanks to a last-minute free kick against Greece that took England to the 2002 World Cup. The England fans would never forget that.

That was a goal that took real guts, one of David's greatest strengths – along with, of course, his remarkable right foot.

CHAPTER 2

MANCHESTER UNITED MAD

'What do you think, son?' Ted asked with a proud smile on his face. 'I think red really suits you!'

David giggled, threw his little arms up in the air, and ran around the room in circles.

'I think he agrees!' his mum Sandra laughed from behind the video camera.

Ted was a huge football fan. Although the Beckham family lived in London, he didn't support Tottenham or Arsenal, or Chelsea or West Ham. No, he was Manchester United mad, and he often travelled up to Old Trafford to watch his favourite team play.

When it came to his son's third birthday, Ted knew exactly what to buy him – his first Manchester United kit.

'You're never too young to become a Red Devil,' Ted told his wife. 'Plus, your father is trying to turn him into a Spurs fan and we can't have that!'

The shirt looked a little big on David, but he'd soon grow into it. Then, once he'd grown out of that one, he'd get another one, perhaps with his favourite player's name on the back. And soon, he'd be ready for his first trip to Old Trafford. Ted couldn't wait to take his son to his first match.

'You're going to love it there, son. It's the Theatre of Dreams!'

Ted still played football for a team called Kingfisher in the local league but once upon a time, he'd had trials with Leyton Orient. He was a big, tough striker but he never quite had the speed or skill to make it as a professional. Now, he hoped that maybe his football dream could become his son's football dream.

'He's going to be the next Bobby Charlton!' Ted told everyone confidently.

David's football journey had started as soon as he could walk. His dad dropped balls at his feet and then stood back and watched.

'Go on, kick!' Ted cheered lovingly, swinging his leg through the air to demonstrate.

When David picked the ball up with his hands instead, his dad didn't lose hope. 'Perhaps he'll be United's next goalkeeper!' he thought to himself.

Soon, however, David learnt to kick, and once he started kicking, he never stopped kicking. He was a natural. He kicked anything and everything in his path – footballs, tennis balls, stones, socks... even his sister Lynne's Care Bear toys.

'Mum!' Lynne cried out from the top of the stairs. 'David's doing it again!'

Now that he had his first Manchester United shirt, it was even harder to stop him kicking. He raced around the living room, wearing holes in the carpet. Luckily, he couldn't do too much damage with a small, soft ball.

'*Gooooooooooooooooooooaaaaaaaaaaaaaaaaallllllllllll llllllllllllllll!!!!!!!!!!!!!!!!!!!*' David cheered.

'Okay, that's enough – you're going to make yourself dizzy!' Sandra warned him gently. 'Why doesn't Daddy take you out into the back garden for a bit of fresh air?'

'Good idea!' Ted replied happily.

It was a bright, sunny May afternoon and there was a ball out there waiting for them. Their kickabout started softly, but David's kicks were getting more and more powerful.

'That's it, son!' his dad cheered, urging him on. He could see it now, his son scoring at Old Trafford. 'Try kicking it even harder!'

'No, no, no – stop!' Sandra groaned loudly. She should have known better than to let them loose in her garden. Even from the back door, she could see the damage. Her beautiful flowerbeds were flattened and ruined.

David looked up at her with big, innocent eyes. 'Mummy, what's wrong? Do you want to play too? One day, I'll play for Man U!' he said proudly, pointing down at his muddy red shirt.

His mum's anger disappeared straight away. How could she argue with that?

'Sorry,' her husband said guiltily, picking up the football. 'We got a little carried away, didn't we, David? Come on son, we'll go and play in the park instead!'

CHAPTER 3

PRACTICE MAKES PERFECT

Chase Lane Park was just around the corner from their house. It was David's favourite place in the world, a football fantasy land. There were big, empty grass pitches with white line markings and real goal posts. What more could you want?

'Slow down!' Ted called out. He had to walk quickly just to keep up with his excited son.

At the beginning, David just dribbled past imaginary defenders and took shots against his dad. That was really fun but by the age of six, he was ready for something a little more serious.

'Dad, if I want to play for Manchester United one day, what do I need to do?' David asked with a focused look on his young face.

Ted smiled and clapped his hands. It was the question that he'd been hoping for. 'Well, son, let me show you!'

He kicked the ball high up into the air and told David to control it. 'Watch it carefully,' Ted said, 'all the way onto your boot!'

At first, the ball went everywhere, no matter how carefully David watched it. It bounced off his shin, it rolled off his boot, and sometimes it even missed his boot completely. But eventually, he managed to trap the ball nicely and pass it back to his dad. David was delighted. He thought his first lesson was over, but he thought wrong.

'Good, now try another ten,' Ted called out. 'Practice makes perfect!'

The next lesson was striking the ball. David thought he was already quite good at that, but it turned out he still had a lot to learn. His dad stood there, tall and wide, between David and the goal.

'Try to score!' Ted challenged him.

The only way to score was to bend the ball around

him. That took hours and hours of practice, but David kept going, even when his legs ached, and when night was falling around them.

'I can do this,' he told himself.

Sometimes, when things weren't going well, David wished his dad would just go in goal and let him shoot, like the other parents at Chase Lane Park. But most of the time, he was grateful for Ted's help. He couldn't make it all the way to Manchester United on his own.

David's striking technique was unique, but also very successful. He placed the ball down and took six steps back. As he ran up, he swung his left arm backwards and his right foot forwards to get maximum power. He kicked it with the side of his big toe to get extra curl and spin as it flew around his dad and into the net.

'Good, now try another ten,' Ted called out, again. 'Practice makes perfect!'

Even when his dad was away at work, David still went down to Chase Lane Park. It was where he always wanted to be. If there were other kids around, he asked to join in their games. David was usually quite a shy child, but football gave him the confidence to talk to the big boys. Some of them were double his age and most of them were double his skinny size.

'Sure! What's your name? Everyone, this is David. Neil, he's on your team now!'

David enjoyed testing his talent in proper matches, especially against bigger, stronger kids. Whenever he took a knock, he just got up and got on with the game, just like his dad had always taught him. If he got tackled, it meant that he needed to think faster.

'Look for the space,' he kept telling himself.

If he was on his own, David just practised his shots and passes. There was a small hut in the corner of Chase Lane Park, with wire covering the windows. He aimed for that wire again and again and each time he hit it, he moved a little bit further away. That way, his accuracy was improving all the time.

Most people would have found that boring and repetitive, but not David. Hours would fly by and he would still be having fun. His dad's words were always there in his head – 'Practice makes perfect'.

By the age of seven, David had a new favourite place. Wadham Lodge was the home of Kingfisher, his dad's team. It was no Old Trafford, but it was a better football fantasy land than Chase Lane Park. There were goal nets, changing rooms, dugouts and even floodlights.

'This place is amazing!' David marvelled out loud. 'One day, I'm going to play here.'

Whenever his dad would let him, he went along to training and they kicked a ball around on the pitch before and after the session. David loved watching all of the emotion and drama on display. Competitive football looked so exciting. By the end, he couldn't wait for his turn to play. Once everyone else had gone home, it was free-kick time. David placed the ball down outside the penalty area and stepped back to strike it.

'Right, I'll give you 50p for every time you hit the crossbar,' Ted challenged his son.

Challenge accepted and soon, challenge completed! Even as a young kid, David was earning money with his remarkable right foot.

CHAPTER 4

RIDGEWAY ROVERS

When David was eight, his dad stopped playing for Kingfisher. As much as Ted loved playing football, he couldn't go on forever. His creaking body wouldn't let him, so he focused on coaching instead, and coaching one youngster in particular.

'Taxi driver at your service,' Ted joked to David, pretending to bow.

By then, David was playing so much football that his parents could barely keep up. He was playing for Chase Lane Primary School and the Cubs, as well as all the friendly matches at Chase Lane Park and Wadham Lodge. If there was a game going on, David would be there as fast as his little legs could carry him.

'Don't you ever get bored?' his younger sister,

Joanne, asked him. She liked following her brother around, but it was always just football, football and more football. It was so dull.

'No, never!' he replied as if it was the silliest question in the world. He couldn't get enough.

One day, Ted saw an advert in the local newspaper for a new boys' team called Ridgeway Rovers. They were holding trials around the corner in Chase Lane Park.

'What do you think?' he asked, showing it to his son.

'Let's go!' David said straight away.

Stuart Underwood was the manager of the Ridgeway Rovers. He knew that there were lots of talented young players in the neighbourhood and his dream was to bring them together and turn them into a really good team. As he laid out the cones and sorted the bibs, Stuart started to feel a little anxious.

What if no-one turned up?

Not a problem! There were already a few boys kicking a ball around with his son, Robert.

Okay, well what if all the kids turned out to be

terrible?

Not a problem! With the right kind of coaching, Stuart would turn them into world-beaters.

'Welcome, everyone!' Stuart's voice boomed across the park. He was a big guy and some of the kids looked terrified as he loomed over them. 'Thanks for coming along this afternoon. Right, let's have some fun!'

David had lots of fun. He loved showing off his excellent ball control and passing range, especially on home soil at Chase Lane Park. All of those hours with his dad had prepared him well.

When he got a little over-confident, Stuart told him so. 'Keep it simple, kid. We're not Brazil – not yet, anyway!'

In his head, however, the Ridgeway Rovers manager was thinking, 'Wow, he's special!' The kid had great technique, but he also had a great attitude. Stuart could see that David was eager to learn and improve. 'That's it – lovely!' he said, encouragingly.

Even in that very first practice, David made lots of new friends. Robert, Ryan, Steve, Jason, Micah, Chris

– they were all good players and a good laugh too.

'Dad, please can I join?' David asked eagerly at the end.

When it came to football, Ted could never say no, and soon he was even one of Ridgeway's coaches.

'Don't expect an easy ride just because you're my son,' he warned.

David smiled. 'Dad, you've been coaching me all my life! Don't worry, I know what to expect. I'm ready to work twice as hard as the other boys.'

To get everyone up to speed, Ridgeway ran two training sessions a week. Stuart was firm but fair with his players. His rules were simple. If you didn't turn up for training, you didn't play at the weekend. If you weren't giving 110 per cent effort on the pitch, you were taken off.

'It's all about commitment,' their manager told them.

David's commitment was never in doubt. He was preparing himself to one day become a professional. He never stopped believing.

The hard work and team spirit soon paid off, as

the Ridgeway Rovers took the local league by storm.
After a couple of seasons, they were winning every
trophy up for grabs.

'Boys, you're the best team that I could ever ask
for,' Stuart told them proudly.

David loved every minute of it. He was Ridgeway's
wing wizard, whipping in excellent crosses all game,
every game. He swung his left arm backwards and
his remarkable right foot forwards. Boom! He curled
the ball into the box and straight onto Chris's head.

*Goooooooooooooooooooooaaaaaaaaaaaaaaaaallllllllllll
llllllllllllll!!!!!!!!!!!!!!!!!!!!*

But the more goals David set up, the more tough
tackles and crafty kicks came his way. As one of the
smallest players on the pitch, it was the easiest way
to keep him quiet.

'Arghhhhhh!' he cried out.

David always tried to get up and get on with the
game, just like his dad had always taught him, but
that wasn't always possible. Sometimes, the boy left
the pitch in so much pain that he had to miss the
next match. A week without football was the worst

thing ever. What could he do to avoid the injuries?

'Sometimes, you've got to release the ball early,' Ted taught him in the park. 'Pass and move, pass and move. Defenders will find it harder to foul you if you've already passed it on to the next player!'

As ever, David listened carefully and learnt his lessons quickly. It was all part of his big plan – to become a professional footballer and make it all the way to Manchester United.

For now, however, he already had offers to train with four London clubs: West Ham, Wimbledon, Arsenal and Tottenham. In the end, David chose Tottenham.

'Just you wait until Grandad hears the news,' his mum said. 'He'll be so proud of you!'

David was proud of himself too. He had earned this amazing opportunity at a top English club. It was just a shame that it wasn't Manchester United. Even on his first day at Tottenham, he refused to hide his favourite team. He ignored his mum's advice and wore his red shirt to White Hart Lane.

'You do know you're at Spurs, right?' asked their

brilliant young defender, Sol Campbell, during the warm-up.

David nodded. His grandad had bought him lots of Tottenham shirts when he was younger, but he would always be a Red Devil.

'You're either very brave or very stupid!' their skilful midfielder Nick Barmby added with a grin.

CHAPTER 5

MOVING TO MANCHESTER UNITED

Manchester United had a team of scouts spread out all over the country. Malcolm Fidgeon was their man in London and he had a very busy job. There was no way that he could watch every talented youngster in the city, but he gave it his best shot.

One day, Malcolm was at an Under-12s game between Redbridge and Waltham Forest. He had heard wonderful things about one of Waltham Forest's young players, a small winger with a remarkable right foot.

'Let's see what you've got, kid,' the scout muttered under his breath as the match kicked off.

Malcolm was ready to be disappointed. Manchester United were only looking for the very best players, kids with amazing talent *and* the right attitude. Time and time again, he saw one but not the other.

Sometimes, Malcolm found skilful players who just wanted to show off. Not good enough! Sometimes, Malcolm found hard-working players who just wanted to run. Not good enough!

Discovering 'a Manchester United player' was like a treasure hunt. There were lots of twists and wrong-turns along the way, but it was all totally worth it in the end.

Fortunately, with Malcolm watching, David played one of the best games of his life. He was everywhere. In attack, he used his full range of passes and crosses to drive Waltham Forest forward and set up goals. There was plenty of skill but no showing off. Every touch was calm, clever and accurate.

'An eleven-year-old kid who can play a perfect thirty-yard pass,' Malcolm noted in his head. 'Now that's special!'

In defence, David worked hard for his team, tracking back to stop the Redbridge left-back. Despite his small size, he battled bravely to win every ball.

As he came to the touchline to take a throw-in, Malcolm could see the total focus on his face.

The scout was blown away. 'That kid is a Manchester United player!' he decided, even before half-time.

At full time, Malcolm went over to introduce himself to David's mum. 'Hi there, I work for Manchester United,' he began.

That was enough to give Sandra goosebumps. She tried to listen carefully, but she was too excited to take everything in.

'Your son is exactly the kind of player that we're looking for,' Malcolm went on, 'and I'd like him to come to Manchester for a trial.'

David drifted slowly out of the dressing room as usual. As he got into the car, he looked over at his mum's beaming face.

'What's going on?' he asked.

'You picked a good day to play like that!' Sandra told him. She looked like she was about to burst.

'Why?'

His mum pointed out of the window. 'That man

BECKHAM

over there is a Manchester United scout!'

David checked that it wasn't a cruel joke and then punched the air with joy. He had been waiting so long to hear those words, so long that he had started to think that it might never happen. But now his dream was finally coming true! He wanted to share his news with the whole world, but with one person in particular.

'When we get home, can I call Dad?' he asked.

Malcolm drove David up to Manchester himself. At first, they didn't say much but three hours was a long time to sit in silence, and so they began to make small talk.

'Have you been to Old Trafford before?' Malcolm asked.

David nodded. 'I played on the pitch last year, actually.'

The scout seemed surprised. 'What competition was that?'

'The Bobby Charlton Soccer School skills competition. We went on before the United vs Spurs game and there must have been about forty thousand people watching us.'

'Well, this trial should be a walk in the park, then!' Malcolm laughed.

Soon enough, David would be involved in another United vs Spurs battle.

David had the time of his life, playing football, football and more football. Luckily, his energy was endless. The trip made him even more certain about moving to Manchester United.

'Dad, it's unbelievable here!' he raved on the phone. When he got home, he couldn't stop talking about his Old Trafford adventure.

After that first trial, David was called back for another one, and then another one. He had clearly impressed the coaches, but had he done enough to join their youth team permanently? That was the big question that gave David sleepless nights.

A few weeks later, the home phone rang. Ted answered it and when he returned, he looked like he'd seen a ghost.

'Who was it, Dad?' David asked.

'That was Alex Ferguson himself,' Ted replied,

hardly able to believe his own words. 'He said that you're exactly the kind of player that Manchester United are looking for.'

David jumped up off the sofa and ran around the room in circles like he was three years old again. Back then, he had been excited about his first Manchester United shirt. Now, he was excited about his first Manchester United contract. It was an incredible feeling to know that his favourite club in the world wanted him.

'So, what happens now?' he asked his dad. 'When do I sign?'

Ted shrugged. 'I'm not sure, son.'

Thankfully, Manchester United didn't lose interest in David. The club invited him and his parents to a team dinner in London. David sat near Ferguson for the whole meal, waiting for the right moment to give him his gift. Finally, he plucked up the courage.

'Wow, thanks, David,' the manager said, taking the pen out of its box. 'What a lovely gift! I'm going to use this pen to sign you for Manchester United.'

David's smile lasted days. He just wished that he

had recorded Ferguson's amazing words. Luckily, he had remembered them off by heart to tell his friends.

As his thirteenth birthday drew near, David had a decision to make. He was enjoying himself at Tottenham and they offered him a brilliant six-year deal. By the age of eighteen, he would be a professional footballer.

'So, are you ready to sign?' the Tottenham manager Terry Venables asked him.

David paused. He knew that it would make his grandad happy, but he needed to hear Manchester United's offer first. 'I'd like to think about it, please.'

After a quick handshake, Ferguson got straight down to business. 'We want to offer you a six-year deal,' he announced.

David looked over at his dad, who looked like he was about to collapse with shock and pride.

'I want to sign,' David said quickly. He didn't need time to think it over. This was the only club for him.

Ferguson smiled and took out the pen that David had given him as a gift. 'Welcome to Manchester United!'

CHAPTER 6

THE CLASS OF '92

Signing for Manchester United was a big step for David, but it was still only the first step. David was only thirteen and he still had a long journey ahead of him if he wanted to achieve his dream of playing for the first team.

'Don't start thinking you've made it yet,' his dad liked to remind him.

For the next two years, David stayed at home in London, playing football for Ridgeway Rovers as normal. Malcolm was there to keep an eye on him and report back to Old Trafford.

'I hope you told Fergie about that free kick I scored!' David told him with a cheeky grin.

It was only during the school holidays that he spent time in Manchester. The club invited him to come up for training camps.

'How long can I stay?' David asked eagerly. 'A month? Six weeks?'

Malcolm laughed. 'Sorry, it's just a week this time!'

Going away for the summer was fun, but going away for good? That was a lot tougher, but when he turned fifteen, it was time for David to leave home.

'Remember, you can call us at any time,' Sandra told him, trying not to cry in front of him. 'Day or night!'

'Enjoy yourself, son!' Ted said, giving him a hearty hug.

At times, David did miss his family, but they came up to watch him play every weekend. And normally, he was too busy enjoying himself to think of home. When he wasn't playing football, he was going to the cinema and hanging out with his new mates.

All of the boys who weren't from Manchester lived together in boarding houses. They had a landlady who looked after them, but most of the time, they were free to explore. There was John O'Kane from Nottingham, Robbie Savage from Wales, and Keith Gillespie all the way from Ireland.

'If we stick together, maybe the other lads won't make fun of our accents!' they decided.

Those other lads included a group who had played together for years at a local team called Boundary Park. The Neville brothers, Gary and Phil, played in defence, Nicky Butt played in midfield and Paul Scholes was an attacker. They were a tight-knit bunch but, thanks to football, David was soon allowed to join their gang.

'Here comes the London lad again!' they liked to joke, putting on awful Cockney voices.

'Thanks, now I feel right at home!' David joked back.

As soon as training started, however, the laughter stopped. The Manchester United youth coach, Eric Harrison, was like Stuart, David's manager at Ridgeway Rovers. He expected 100 per cent effort and commitment at all times.

'There are millions of kids out there who would love to be in your position,' Eric told his young stars. 'Don't waste this chance!'

If anyone dared to mess around, they were in big trouble. Even if he wasn't there with them on the field, Eric was usually watching them through the window of his office. If he saw something he didn't like, he would bang furiously on the glass.

That sound was something the players all dreaded. 'Uh-oh!' they'd say, looking down at their feet guiltily.

Eric knew how to get the best out of each and every one of them. He was always looking for ways to improve his young players and help them to achieve their full potential. Eric wasn't worried about David's work rate. He knew that he would run up and down the wing all day long in order to win a football match.

Instead, Eric worked on his decision making. Sometimes, the simple pass was the best pass, rather than trying to strike it sixty yards. David's midfield hero was England's classy playmaker, Glenn Hoddle, but football couldn't always be that beautiful.

'Stop going for those Hollywood balls every time!' Eric shouted angrily on the touchline.

When the practice finished, he went over to offer David more advice. 'Get the basics right first. Watch Bryan Robson – watch what he does.'

With Eric's guidance and Robson's example, David got better and better. He still loved playing long passes but he had to pick the right moments to use that remarkable right foot of his.

Gary Neville was just as determined and they often stayed behind to do extra practice together. After training in the morning and training in the afternoon, they would then train with the schoolboys in the evening.

'You lads will go far with an attitude like that!' Eric told them.

That was exactly what they were hoping. Another Manchester United youngster, Ryan Giggs, was already on his way to becoming a first-team star. That gave David and Gary the confidence to keep chasing their dream.

David needed that self-belief because he had a battle on his hands. Keith played on the right wing too and in the big FA Youth Cup matches, he was Eric's first choice. How could David force his way into the starting line-up? By doing what he always did – working hard and creating goals.

Eventually, Eric had no option but to move Keith up front and bring David into the team. After playing well against Tottenham in the semi-final, he stayed there for the final against Crystal Palace.

'Yes!' David shouted when he saw his name there on the teamsheet, alongside Gary, John, Robbie and Nicky. 'Come on, let's win this, lads!'

On a soaking wet Selhurst Park pitch, Nicky gave Manchester United the lead. Then, after thirty minutes, the ball came towards David on the edge of the penalty area. There was no time to think or take a touch. He smashed a vicious left-foot volley past the keeper.

Goooooooooooooooooooooaaaaaaaaaaaaaaaaalllllllllllll llllllllllllllll!!!!!!!!!!!!!!!!!!!!!

It took a moment to sink in but once it did, it

was the greatest moment of David's life. Adrenaline flooded his body and he felt like he could run forever. He raced towards the corner, with his teammates chasing behind.

'Becks, I didn't even know you had a left foot!' Gary teased as they celebrated.

For the second leg at Old Trafford, they had 30,000 fans cheering them on. Word was spreading about the club's amazing 'Class of '92'.

'Don't get ahead of yourselves, they're just here to see me!' Giggsy joked. He was back to captain the team to victory.

Once it started, David didn't want the match to ever end. What a night! The atmosphere was amazing. He was playing football with his friends for his favourite club in the world in front of a roaring crowd. Could life get any better than that?

Yes, with a trophy! As Giggsy lifted the FA Youth Cup high into the sky, David stood right behind him. When it was David's turn, he raised it towards his proud parents. He had so much to thank them for.

'This is the best youth team I've ever worked with,' Eric told the media.

Alex Ferguson was there at Old Trafford too to congratulate the Class of '92. In the dressing room, he looked around at the future first-team stars – Giggsy, Gary, Nicky and David. The right winger wasn't the most highly-rated member of the team, but Ferguson could see the pure ambition in his eyes.

'That boy is going to be a top, top player,' the Manchester United manager thought to himself.

CHAPTER 7

TESTING TIMES

After his key role in Manchester United's FA Youth Cup victory, David looked destined for the big time. How long would it be before he joined the first team?

David made his senior team debut a few months later in the League Cup against Brighton and Hove Albion. With twenty minutes to go, he came on to replace Andrei Kanchelskis on the right wing.

'Run your socks off and get some crosses into the box,' Ferguson instructed him.

David did exactly that. By the final whistle, he was exhausted, but his whole body was buzzing. He could really call himself a Manchester United player now.

'How was it?' his dad asked.

David didn't have the words to describe the feeling. 'Unbelievable!' he went for in the end, but it didn't do it justice.

When David signed his first professional contract in January 1993, he could see his Manchester United journey in front of him. From the youth team, he would go to the reserves, then to the first team squad, and finally to the starting line-up.

In his head, it was going to be a rapid rise, but it didn't turn out that way. He would have to wait two whole years to make his full debut.

In the meantime, he played lots of games for the reserves and he played in a second FA Youth Cup Final. He lined up in midfield with Nicky. Gary was the captain at the back, and Paul Scholes was up front.

'Let's win this, lads!' Gary shouted confidently.

It looked like another strong Manchester United team, but they were no match for Leeds. Wearing the Number 8 shirt, David did his best to create chances for his team, but it was difficult on a boggy, bobbling pitch. Every time he crossed the ball into the box, the big Leeds defenders headed it away.

'Simple passes!' Eric screamed on the touchline.

At the final whistle, David trudged off through the mud. It was a year on from their success against Crystal Palace, and it didn't feel like he was getting any closer to the first team. These were testing times for a young footballer.

'Be patient,' his dad told him. 'You've only just turned eighteen!'

'I know, but Giggsy is already playing week in, week out for the first team. When am I going to get my chance?'

'Trust me, you'll get your chance soon, son.'

The 1993–94 season came and went but as the next season arrived, things were looking up for David. Ferguson gave him his first start in the League Cup against Port Vale. There were four members of the Class of '92 on the teamsheet – David, Nicky, Gary and Scholesy. It was their big chance to shine and impress their manager.

'We need to do a better job than we did against

Leeds,' Gary said on the way to the game.

'That won't be hard, especially for you!' Nicky joked back.

On the night, Scholesy was United's hero with two brilliant goals. David was really pleased for his friend, but he couldn't help feeling a little bit jealous too. With Fergie watching on, he had failed to be his team's stand-out star. The others were leaving him behind.

Would David get another chance? He played in the next round against Newcastle, but they lost 2–0.

And another? In December, he was in the squad for the Champions League game against Galatasaray. There were rumours in the newspapers that the manager was going to give his youngsters a chance, but David didn't want to get his hopes up. It was best to assume that he was on the bench.

That all changed on match day, however, when Ferguson read out the teamsheet:

'...Number Seven: Cantona, Eight: Butt, Nine:. McClair, Ten: Beckham, Eleven: Davies...'

'We're starting!' Nicky whispered happily.

David couldn't believe it. His parents were going to be in the crowd but there was no time to tell them the exciting news. So they were in for a shock when they saw their son walking out at Old Trafford with Steve Bruce, Denis Irwin, Brian McClair and Eric Cantona.

Suddenly, David was very nervous about making his European debut. What if he missed an important tackle, or gave the ball away for Galatasaray to score?

'Good luck, lad,' Roy Keane said, giving him a slap on the back. 'Show the fans what you're made of!'

Brian chased after a long goal kick, but a defender slid in for the tackle. As the ball bounced out to the edge of the penalty area, David sprinted towards it as fast as he could. He won the race and shot past the diving goalkeeper.

Goooooooooooooooooooaaaaaaaaaaaaaaaaalllllllllllll llllllllllllll!!!!!!!!!!!!!!!!!!!!

The ball seemed to roll into back of the net in slow motion. Surely, it was too good to be true? But no, it was true – David had scored in his first ever

Champions League game. His smile kept growing bigger and bigger. Before he knew what he was doing, he was jumping into Eric's arms. Luckily, his French teammate didn't seem to mind.

David came back down to earth with a bang. A few weeks after scoring at Old Trafford, he was off to play for Preston North End in the Third Division.

'You're just going there on loan for a month,' Ferguson reassured him. 'Hopefully, it will toughen you up a bit. Think of it as a valuable experience and a chance to get some more games under your belt. You'll be back here in no time!'

David couldn't help worrying about his United future, but he had to trust his manager and focus on impressing at Preston. He didn't get off to a good start, however.

'This is David Beckham, he's on loan from Manchester United,' the manager, Gary Peters, told his team. 'He'll be taking all our free kicks and corners from now on.'

The senior players weren't happy at all. When David came on for his debut against Doncaster, Paul

Raynor had to come off. He sat down moodily on the bench. 'Who does that kid think he is?' he muttered to himself.

A few minutes later, David swung a high corner all the way into the net.

Goooooooooooooooooooooaaaaaaaaaaaaaaaaaalllllllllllll llllllllllllll!!!!!!!!!!!!!!!!!!!

In his second game, David curled one of his trademark free kicks up over the wall and into the top corner.

Goooooooooooooooooooooaaaaaaaaaaaaaaaaaalllllllllllll llllllllllllll!!!!!!!!!!!!!!!!!!!

After that, Raynor kept quiet. Everyone at Preston could see that David was the real deal. It wasn't just his good looks and natural talent; it was also all the hard work that he did on the training ground. Every day, he stayed behind to do extra practice – free kicks, corners, passes.

'Teacher's pet,' the players called him.

It was all friendly banter, though. On the way to one game, David was sat on his own, reading an article about himself in *Match* magazine, when

Raymond Sharp looked over and snatched it out of his hands.

'Hey, give it back!'

'"Scoring in Europe was a moment that I will never forget",' Sharp read out loud for everyone to enjoy. He even tried to imitate David's London accent. '"When the ball crossed the line, I ran into Eric's arms. It was wonderful."'

David's face was bright red as laughter rang out all over the team bus. Sharp handed the magazine back to him with a wink. 'Just remember us when you're winning the Premier League!'

After two goals in five games, it was time for David to return to Manchester United. 'Good luck, guys!' he called out to the Preston players as he waved goodbye.

'Thanks, we're going to need it without you!' the players replied.

Back at Old Trafford, David finally made his Premier League debut in April 1995 against Leeds United. Even a dull 0–0 draw couldn't dampen his spirits.

'I can't believe I played the full ninety minutes!' he told his parents proudly.

'Fergie must be impressed!' his mum replied, sounding just as proud.

David's confidence grew with more game time against Leicester City, Chelsea and Coventry City. He was almost a regular now.

Manchester United finished the 1994–95 season without a single trophy. Blackburn won the Premier League and Everton won the FA Cup. There was lots of gloom around Old Trafford that summer, but David was feeling positive. His time had arrived.

CHAPTER 8

FERGIE'S FLEDGLINGS

Just as the 1995–96 Premier League season started, Andrei Kanchelskis left Manchester United to join Everton. The Russian winger was the third senior player to leave that summer, after Paul Ince and Mark Hughes. What was going on at Old Trafford, and why wasn't Ferguson buying new players to replace them?

The answer was that the Manchester United manager believed in his new young stars, the Class of '92. He believed that there was no need to replace Ince and Kanchelskis when he already had Giggsy, Scholesy, Nicky and David. The club's future looked very bright indeed.

With Kanchelskis gone, David was now only battling with Lee Sharpe for the right-wing spot.

'This is going to be my season,' David told Gary Neville confidently. 'I know it!'

In the first match against Aston Villa, it was Lee who started alongside Gary, Phil, Nicky and Scholesy. David was disappointed to be the one on the bench, but at half-time, United were losing 3–0.

'Get ready, kid,' Ferguson told him. 'You're coming on.'

David wanted to smile but he didn't. It wasn't a time for smiling; it was a time for focusing. He had forty-five minutes to show that he was good enough to start the next match. He ran and ran, covering every blade of grass on the pitch.

David took the corners, he took the free kicks, and he curled other crosses into the box too. But with ten minutes to go, it was still 3–0 to Aston Villa. When Roy Keane passed to him, David chested the ball down and decided to go for goal. His shot sailed high and wide.

'Hahahaha!' the Villa fans laughed.

But David didn't let that knock his confidence. The next time the ball came to him, he controlled it beautifully, took a touch to steady himself, and then unleashed a powerful, swerving strike.

Mark Bosnich was having a good game in the Villa goal, but he had no chance of saving this one. He could only turn his head to watch it hit the top corner.

Goooooooooooooooooooooaaaaaaaaaaaaaaaallllllllllll llllllllllllll!!!!!!!!!!!!!!!!!!

David was delighted with his first Premier League goal but he didn't really celebrate because United were still losing 3–1. The fans, however, stood and clapped their new scorer. There were just glad to have one positive to take from their team's nightmare start.

'Ferguson needs to buy players,' former Liverpool player Alan Hansen told the British public on *Match of the Day.* 'You can't win anything with kids.'

'We'll see about that!' was the team's response to Hansen's prediction.

After his goal against Aston Villa, David started

the next match and the next and the next. With Eric Cantona and Giggsy missing, the manager played David, Lee and Scholesy in the same attack. 'Fergie's Fledglings' worked brilliantly together.

Against West Ham, Lee played a long pass to Scholesy, who passed to David, who passed to Nicky. Nicky passed to Lee, who flicked it to Keano, who scored. 2–1! As Keano threw himself down on the grass, all of his teammates piled on top of him.

Against Premier League Champions Blackburn, Lee scored the first goal but could United grab the winner too? With the ball bouncing around in the box, it was going to take a moment of calm and class. Up stepped David to curl a first-time shot past the keeper.

Gooooooooooooooooooooaaaaaaaaaaaaaaaaaallllllllllllll llllllllllllllll!!!!!!!!!!!!!!!!!!!!

What an important strike! David threw his arms up in the air and ran towards the United fans by the corner flag. He was having the best time ever.

'You're not just a pretty face!' Keano joked, slapping him playfully on the cheek.

Ferguson ran along the touchline, punching the air. His youngsters were doing him proud.

Things got even better when Giggsy returned. With a Welsh wing wizard on the left and an English wing wizard on the right, United were unstoppable. Giggsy dribbled past defenders for fun and David delivered dangerous cross after cross. Together, they caused so many problems for Premier League defences.

United jumped ahead of Newcastle at the top of the table. It soon became a thrilling two-horse title race – 'Fergie's Fledglings' versus Kevin Keegan's Entertainers. Who would lift the trophy in May? David was as determined as ever. He had achieved his dream of becoming a United player but now, he was on to the next dream – winning trophies.

At Old Trafford, Glenn Hoddle's Chelsea took the lead. It was a match that United couldn't afford to lose because Newcastle were already five points clear. The ball came to David on the edge of the penalty area. He didn't have much time or space to shoot but, in a flash, he lifted the ball over the mass of blue shirts and into the top corner.

*Goooooooooooooooooooooaaaaaaaaaaaaaaaalllllllllllll
lllllllllllllll!!!!!!!!!!!!!!!!!!!!!*

David jumped for joy. At the age of twenty, he was
quickly becoming a key part of the United team.

In the FA Cup semi-final, he scored another
goal against Chelsea and this time, it was the
matchwinner. David chased after Craig Burley's
sloppy back-pass and steered the ball past the keeper.
2–1! The United fans behind the goal bounced up
and down with delight.

'You hero, Becks!' Nicky screamed. 'We're off to
Wembley!'

Before the FA Cup Final, United had a league title
to win. By April, they were top of the table again
and there weren't budging for anyone. David scored
his seventh and eighth goals of the season in a 5–0
thrashing of Nottingham Forest. After that first goal
against Aston Villa, he had never looked back.

'Great, now we just need a draw at
Middlesbrough,' Gary explained. With one point,
United would be crowned champions.

Giggsy shook his head. The Class of '92 didn't

believe in draws. He still remembered that awful draw at West Ham that handed the 1994–95 title to Blackburn. They had to get it right this time. 'No way, we're going for the win as usual!'

Giggsy inspired United to a 3–0 victory. A plane flew over the Riverside Stadium, celebrating the big news: 'MANCHESTER UNITED: CARLING CHAMPIONS'. At the final whistle, 'Fergie's Fledglings' jumped up and down together – they had achieved the impossible!

David had his first senior trophy, the first of many he hoped. What an amazing breakthrough season 1995–96 had been – 39 matches and 8 goals. It was beyond his wildest dreams. He ran over to thank his manager.

'I feel like a very proud father!' Fergie said as his youngsters hugged him. 'I believed in you guys – and boy, did you repay my faith!'

United weren't done yet – the kids had something else to win. They completed The Double at Wembley by beating Liverpool 1–0. As he lifted the FA Cup high above his head, David felt on top of the world.

CHAPTER 9

THE WIMBLEDON WONDERSTRIKE

As the 1996–97 season kicked off, there were so
many questions about the Manchester United team.
Was their Premier League title win from the previous
season a fluke, a one-off? Could they really keep
winning things with kids? And just how good were
'Fergie's Fledglings' anyway?

'Very, very good' was the answer, and they were
only just getting started. David was pleased with
his progress, but one season wasn't enough. He
was determined to go on and establish himself as a
superstar. He was already thinking about his next
dream – playing for England.

After a summer holiday in Italy, he couldn't wait to get back to football.

'The hard work begins today,' Ferguson told his players before the away trip to tough-tackling Wimbledon. 'We're the champions now and that means that everyone is going to want to beat us. Teams are going to try to foul you, cheat you, scare you – anything to win. But don't let them!'

In the tunnel, the Wimbledon captain Vinnie Jones grinned his most fiendish grin. 'Welcome kids, I hope you're ready for this!'

Jones and his 'Crazy Gang' wanted to teach United's skilful youngsters a lesson or two, but David wasn't scared. He was twenty-one years old and fearless. He had been taking on bigger boys for years.

He took his place on the right wing, proudly wearing the United Number 10 shirt. It was a big upgrade from Number 24. He had worked hard to earn it and now it was time to prove that he should keep it. If he didn't, the club's new Czech signing, Karel Poborský, was waiting on the bench.

David's shirt number wasn't the only thing that was new. Adidas had sent him a pair of their latest Predator boots. They looked awesome and they felt awesome, even if they did have the wrong footballer's name written on the red tongues.

'Alright, Charlie!' Nicky joked.

'I can't believe I've been getting your name wrong for all these years,' Scholesy teased. 'Sorry about that, Charlie!'

David laughed along, knowing that a goal would soon shut his friends up.

'Let's do this!' captain Eric roared. He expected 110 per cent effort from his teammates.

With the sun shining brightly, David got stuck in straight away. He raced back to win the ball off Oyvind Leonhardsen and then passed to Keano. Seconds later, it was in the back of the net. 1–0 to United!

As Eric stood and raised his arms up in the air, David, Paul, Nicky and Phil all rushed over to celebrate with their leader. The team was one big, happy family.

With seconds to go, United were cruising to a 2–0 victory. Ronny Johnsen tackled Efan Ekoku and passed to Brian McClair, who poked the ball forward to David just inside his own half. As he looked up for someone to pass to, he spotted that the Wimbledon goalkeeper, Neil Sullivan, was off his line.

'Why not?' David thought to himself.

He had scored lots of long-range goals before and it was a brilliant chance to test his new Predator boots. Surely, Ferguson wouldn't mind him having a go in the last minute of the match?

'Not another Hollywood ball!' David could imagine his old Manchester youth coach shouting.

But he knew that he could do it. He had done it lots of times in training, so why not in a real match? Just before he reached the halfway line, he swung his left arm backwards, and his remarkable right foot forwards. Bang! It looked more like a pass, but that was just David's special, shooting technique. He knew exactly what he was doing.

The stadium fell silent. All eyes watched the ball

as it flew towards the Wimbledon goal. Surely, it couldn't? Could it? It seemed to hang in the air for hours.

At first, Sullivan jogged backwards just in case. But as the ball began to drop, he turned and panicked. He jumped up to try to save it, but he was too late. It landed in the back of the net.

Goooooooooooooooooooooaaaaaaaaaaaaaaaaaalllllllllllll llllllllllllllll!!!!!!!!!!!!!!!!!!!!

The Manchester United fans behind the goal were up on their feet, going wild. They couldn't believe what they had just seen. Their midfielder maestro had just scored from the halfway line!

David stood and raised his arms up in the air like Eric. He tried to look cool, but he couldn't stop the smile from spreading across his face. It was the proudest moment of his career so far. What a way to start the new season!

'Take a bow, David Beckham!' commentator Martin Tyler cheered on TV.

'Charlie, you're a genius!' Scholesy screamed.

Eric was a man of few words but even he went

over to congratulate his teammate. 'What a goal,' he said, with a nod of respect.

David beamed with joy. It meant so much to hear those words from his captain, and his manager's words were even better.

'We've just seen the goal of the season already,' Ferguson told the media. 'I have never seen anyone do that before. Pelé is the only one who came close.'

The next day, the newspapers had a big question for their readers – 'Was That the Greatest Goal Ever?'

David was already a famous face in England, but suddenly, people knew about him all over the world. With that Wimbledon wonderstrike, David took a giant leap towards his dream of becoming a footballing superstar. It was a goal that changed his life forever.

CHAPTER 10

EXCITING NEW ERA FOR ENGLAND

What next for Manchester United's young star? His senior international debut!

After losing to Germany in the semi-finals of Euro 96, England needed some fresh new talent. David fitted the bill perfectly, especially after his recent Wimbledon Wonderstrike. He was a Premier League Champion and a classy midfield playmaker.

'Get Becks in the squad!' the country cried out. 'The World Cup is only two years away!'

The new national team manager was Glenn Hoddle, David's childhood hero. What changes would he make for his first match in charge against Moldova? England were looking to start off their

World Cup qualification campaign with a bang.

David was sat at home, relaxing with his mum, when he checked the football news on TV. Hoddle had just named his squad and his eyes scanned over the names. Gary was in, alongside Stuart Pearce, Gareth Southgate, Paul Ince, David Beckha–

'Mum, look!' David screamed, jumping off the sofa. 'I'm in the England squad!'

After a quick hug, he phoned his dad at work to give him the great news. At first, Ted was speechless.

'Son, that's fantastic!' he managed to say eventually.

Alex Ferguson was delighted too. 'Congratulations! Just play like you've been playing for United, and you'll be fine.'

As he arrived at the national team camp, however, David felt like a little kid again. He was twenty-one years old now but he had grown up watching many of his new international teammates on TV – David Seaman, Paul Gascoigne, Alan Shearer. He felt star-struck.

'Don't just stand there, Becks,' Gary shouted over. 'Get warmed up!'

Once he had the ball at his feet, David remembered Fergie's message – 'Just play like you've been playing for United.'

No problem! With his remarkable right foot, David made sure that every pass and every cross was absolutely perfect. He was so focused on football that he soon forgot who he was playing with.

Hoddle was impressed and named him in the starting line-up. It was an exciting new era for England, and for David.

David thought back to the age of twelve, when a youth coach told him that he would never play for his country.

'Sorry lad, you're too small and weak.'

He thought back to missing out on the England squad for the Under-18 Euros back in 1993.

'Sorry lad, you didn't make the cut this time.'

Those disappointments had only spurred him on to keep going, to keep proving people wrong.

All of that hard work had been worth it. David had progressed from the England Under-18s to the Under-21s, and now he was about to make his senior debut.

'This is amazing!' he told Gary, who was also in the team. 'We're going to rule the right wing!'

In David's childhood dreams, he would have made his debut at Wembley, the Home of Football, in front of 80,000 cheering fans. In reality, there were fewer than 10,000 fans in Moldova's national stadium, but he wore the Three Lions on his shirt and that was all that mattered. After singing the national anthem loud and proud, it was time for David to kick off his England career.

In the end, it was a solid but unspectacular debut. Although he didn't score any wonderstrikes, he looked confident on the ball and never stopped running. With a 3–0 win, David and the exciting new England era were both up and running.

'Well played,' Hoddle said to him at the final whistle. 'How did that feel?'

'Incredible!' David replied, trying to catch his breath.

Now, he just needed to make sure that he kept his place. In the next match against Poland, he dribbled forward, over the halfway line.

'Shoot!' the fans shouted.

Not this time. Instead, he looked up and chipped a long diagonal cross towards Alan Shearer. It was inch-perfect. Alan had the easy job of heading it past the goalkeeper.

'Great ball!' he cheered, giving David a high-five.

It was a real relief to get his first England assist but what about that first England goal? David scored lots of free kicks for his club, so why not for his country?

'You'll get one soon,' Hoddle reassured him in training. 'We've got lots of other goalscorers, though, so don't worry about that. What I want from you is lots of crossing and passing, and you're doing that brilliantly!'

Slowly but surely, Fergie's Fledglings were taking over the England team. By the time Moldova came to Wembley, there were five of them in the team – Gary and Phil in defence, and David, Scholesy and Nicky in midfield. To celebrate, David whipped in a dangerous ball and Scholesy scored with a diving header.

'World Cup, here we come!' David cheered as he

jumped on his Manchester United teammate.

With a hard-fought 0–0 draw in Italy, the Three Lions had qualified for the 1998 World Cup in France. At the final whistle, the players all ran over to celebrate with the supporters.

England! England! England!

What a feeling – David was a national hero now. If he kept playing like he'd been playing for United, he would soon be off to the World Cup in France.

CHAPTER 11

POSH AND BECKS

David was making a name for himself at Manchester United, both on and off the pitch.

On the pitch, David wasn't just scoring goals for his club; he was scoring *brilliant* goals.

Against Derby, he dribbled forward and fired a great shot past the goalkeeper.

Goooooooooooooooooooooaaaaaaaaaaaaaaaaaalllllllllllll llllllllllllll!!!!!!!!!!!!!!!!!!!

Against Southampton, he curled a fierce free kick up over the wall and into the top corner.

Goooooooooooooooooooooaaaaaaaaaaaaaaaaaalllllllllllll llllllllllllll!!!!!!!!!!!!!!!!!!!

And David wasn't just scoring brilliant goals for his

club; he was scoring brilliant and *important* goals. He scored the winners against Liverpool and Tottenham and the equaliser against Chelsea. He was becoming a big game player.

Off the pitch, meanwhile, David was now one half of England's hottest celebrity couple.

The music group, the Spice Girls, had taken the country by storm. There were five members, all with different personalities: Sporty Spice, Scary Spice, Ginger Spice, Baby Spice – and then Posh Spice, Victoria Adams.

Everyone had their favourite Spice Girl, especially David. 'Posh is perfect,' he told Gary as they watched music videos together on TV. 'She's so beautiful and stylish. She's the one for me!'

But how would he get to meet the girl of his dreams? Luckily, after a Manchester United game against Chelsea, David found out that two of the Spice Girls were up in the Players' Lounge.

'Which ones?' he asked frantically.

No-one knew the answer, so he rushed to find out for himself. It turned out to be Posh and Sporty. As he started speaking to them, he was so nervous that he could feel the sweat trickling down his forehead. Playing football in front of 70,000 fans at Old Trafford was nothing compared to this.

'Hello, I'm David,' he said.

'Hello, I'm Victoria,' she said.

And that was it. David froze – he didn't know what to say next. He was tongue-tied, and he couldn't take his eyes off her.

Victoria wasn't much of a football fan, but she was a big fan of David. A week later, she travelled from London to Manchester just to watch a match at Old Trafford. Afterwards, she was there in the Players' Lounge, waiting for him.

When he saw Victoria there, David's heart nearly leapt out of his chest. He stood talking to his parents for a while, trying to calm himself down. The last thing he wanted to do was make a fool of himself for a second time.

Eventually, however, David plucked up the courage to go over and speak to her. He was nervous at first but once he relaxed, they chatted for ages about fame,

their families and growing up in Essex. They had lots
in common and made each other laugh.

This time, before she left to go home, Victoria
asked for David's phone number. He was crazy about
her, but what if she lost the scrap of paper and never
called? He didn't want to take that risk.

'No, I'll take yours,' David decided.

'Okay,' Victoria replied with a smile, writing it on
the back of an old plane ticket. 'Let me know when
you're next in London!'

When he got home, David wrote the number
down in lots of different places, just to be safe. He
called her as soon as he woke up the next day.

'Victoria? It's David.'

For the first few months, David and Victoria
managed to keep their relationship a secret. That
wasn't easy for two famous people, but it gave them
time to really get to know each other. David's phone
bill got bigger and bigger each week, as did the
bouquets of flowers that he sent to Victoria.

'Who's your secret admirer?' her sister Louise asked.

'A guy in Manchester,' was all Victoria would say.

When they went on dates, they chose random places, far from the public eye. No matter where they met, though, David always made sure that his car looked sparkling clean. He was eager to impress Victoria and they spent hours talking over romantic, candlelit dinners.

'We haven't hung out for ages!' Gary complained at training one day.

'Sorry, I've been busy,' David replied.

'Busy with what? You're always in a good mood these days. Have you got a girlfriend?'

David stayed silent.

'You have, haven't you!' Gary teased. 'Who is she, then? Anyone I know?'

Should he just say, 'a girl from London'? No, he wanted to tell his best friend the truth. After another short silence, David revealed his secret. 'Victoria Adams.'

Gary looked confused.

'Posh Spice,' David explained.

Their relationship was soon front page news. Suddenly, the paparazzi followed them everywhere, even when they walked their dogs down the street.

'Posh and Becks' were the talk of the UK.

David had always liked to look stylish but now that he was a celebrity footballer, he had to look stylish all the time. Not only that, but he also had to keep changing his style all the time too. Otherwise, his fans would get bored and move on to a new heartthrob. David started slicking his hair back with gel and then dyed it blonde.

As soon as he arrived at training, his teammates mocked him mercilessly.

'Blimey, I thought this was a sports team, not a boyband!'

'Before you ask, no I'm not joining the Spice Boys!'

'These days, you spend longer in front of the mirror than you do on the football pitch!'

David smiled and laughed along. Just as long as he was playing well for Manchester United, he could do whatever he liked in his private life.

In May 1997, David won his second Premier League title and the PFA Young Player of the Year award. In January 1998, he asked Victoria to marry him. She said yes.

CHAPTER 12

A MOMENT OF MADNESS

With so much media attention on David at home, it was nice for him to escape for the summer. He was off to France, but it wasn't for a holiday – it was for the 1998 World Cup. He couldn't wait to play in his first major international tournament.

Growing up, David had been England's biggest fan. He'd cheered on Bryan Robson and Glenn Hoddle in 1982, Gary Lineker in 1986 and then Gazza in 1990. Eight years on, David was the one representing his country at the World Cup.

'It's going to be awesome!' he told Gary and Scholesy.

Gary had played at Euro 96 but Scholesy had even

fewer England caps than David. The three of them were representing Manchester United's Class of '92. Nicky and Phil hadn't been picked, while Giggsy had chosen to play for Wales instead.

'He'll never admit it, but he must really regret that decision!' Scholesy joked.

England went into the World Cup with high hopes. There was lots of talent and experience in the team's core – David Seaman in goal, Tony Adams in defence, Paul Ince in midfield and Alan Shearer in attack.

But Hoddle had also picked lots of exciting young players. Fergie's Fledglings were joined by Tottenham's Sol Campbell, West Ham's Rio Ferdinand and, most exciting of all, Liverpool's eighteen-year-old striker Michael Owen.

'I'm glad he's on our team this time,' Gary admitted. 'He's absolutely rapid!'

David and Gary were both on the bench for the first game against Tunisia. Darren Anderton played at right wing-back, putting them both out of a position. They watched and waited, melting in the Marseille heat. But their chance never came because Alan and Scholesy scored to give England the victory.

'What a strike, mate!' David congratulated his friend.

'Yeah, but what about that miss in the first-half, Scholesy?' Gary teased.

Hoddle brought Gary into the team against Romania, but he still left David on the bench. This wasn't how he'd imagined his first World Cup, especially as he had played every single qualifying game. After thirty minutes, however, Paul Ince injured his ankle. He had to go off, but who would come on to replace him? David!

David tucked in his baggy Number 7 shirt and ran on to the field. He had achieved yet another childhood dream – playing for England at the World Cup. But before he could really get into the game, Romania took the lead.

'Come on!' Seaman cried out in frustration.

David did his best to set up the equaliser. He kept putting balls into the box for Alan and Teddy Sheringham to attack. The crosses were excellent, of course, but the goal didn't arrive. With twenty minutes to go, Michael came on for Teddy. Suddenly, England had some pace to play with.

David dribbled forward and played a great pass over the top to Alan. Alan smashed the ball across goal, but Scholesy couldn't quite control it. Luckily, Michael was right behind and ready to score. 1–1!

David raced over to hug England's goalscoring hero. 'What a super sub!' he cheered.

Michael grinned. 'Yeah and so are you. They've got to start us next time!'

Before that, however, Romania scored again to win the game. That meant England would have to beat Colombia in their final group game or be knocked out of the tournament.

'We can't let that happen!' captain Alan demanded.

Hoddle finally made the attacking changes that the English people were calling for. In came David and Michael to play with Alan, Scholesy and Darren. 'Go score some goals!' their manager shouted.

After twenty minutes, Darren slammed a rocket of

a shot into the roof of the net. 1–0! He ran over to David to celebrate.

'See Becks, of course we can play in the same team!'

Ten minutes later, England won a free kick in a good shooting position. David still hadn't scored for England, but his teammates believed in him. 'You've got this!' Darren told him.

'Yes, I've got this!' David told himself. He took a deep breath and imagined that he was back at Old Trafford, scoring another Premier League free kick. If he could do it there, he could do it anywhere.

As David ran forward, he swung his left arm backwards and his remarkable right foot forwards. Bang! The ball curled up over the wall and then dipped down into the bottom corner.

Gooooooooooooooooooooaaaaaaaaaaaaaaaaalllllllllllllll llllllllllllll!!!!!!!!!!!!!!!!!!!

What a way for David to score his first England goal! He had been waiting a long time for this moment. How should he celebrate? He raced over to the fans behind the goal and stood in front of them, pumping his fists. Finally, his teammates caught up with him and Gary jumped up onto his back.

'Mate, that was unstoppable!' he cheered.

This was how David had imagined his first World Cup, full of goals and glory.

Next up in the second round, England faced their old rivals, Argentina. There was no question that David would start – he was the new national hero.

It turned out to be one of the most thrilling matches of the tournament. After ten minutes, it was already 1–1. David fed a great pass through for Michael to chase. The speedy striker was off, dribbling forward, past defender after defender. In the box, he finished off his wondergoal in style. 2–1 to England!

'You beauty!' David screamed.

It was all going so well for England. Too well. Just before half time, Argentina made it 2–2. Then just after half time, David went to chest the ball down, but Diego Simeone barged right into his back.

'Arghhhhh!' David cried out.

He was furious about the foul. As he lay on the floor, he kicked out at the Argentina midfielder's legs. It was a moment of madness, right in front of the referee. Simeone collapsed to the floor and David was off. Red card!

What a mistake. He could see the disappointment on his teammates' faces – Alan, Scholesy, Gary. But he hadn't just let them down – he had let his whole country down.

He didn't argue. He just turned and traipsed off the pitch. It was the longest walk of his life. He could feel so many eyes watching him, despising him for what he had just done. He deserved it.

'What was I thinking? I did exactly what Simeone hoped I would do. I'm so stupid!'

England's ten men held on, all the way to penalties but in the shoot-out, Incey and David Batty both missed. They were out of the World Cup.

David sat there in the dressing room, crying on his own, waiting for his teammates to return. What would they say? At first, there was total silence. Gary and Scholesy came over and patted him on the back but no-one said a word. Finally, Tony put an arm around him and spoke.

'Look son, everyone makes mistakes,' he said. 'You're going to come back bigger and better, I promise.'

Those kind words meant a lot to him, but David was distraught. In the space of four days, he had gone from national hero to national villain.

'Ten Heroic Lions, One Stupid Boy,' one newspaper headline read.

As seemingly the most hated man in England, David was dreading his return from France. He would have to face horrible abuse, both through his letter box and in stadiums across the country. How was he going to deal with all that anger? He couldn't do it on his own. At that difficult time in his life, he needed support.

As soon as he finished speaking to his parents and Victoria, his phone rang again. It was his manager and mentor.

'Son, get back to Manchester,' Ferguson told him calmly. 'We'll look after you. You'll be fine.'

CHAPTER 13

THE TREBLE

Fergie was right – David would be fine. He just needed to focus on his football – winning more trophies with Manchester United, and then making things right with England.

'You're made of strong stuff,' his dad reminded him. 'Come back even stronger!'

David did just that. In the last minute of the first match of the 1998–99 season, Manchester United were losing 2–1. They won a free kick within shooting range.

'Is this going to be David Beckham's big moment?' the TV commentator asked.

Yes! The ball swerved and dipped into the bottom corner.

*Gooooooooooooooooooooaaaaaaaaaaaaaaaaalllllllllll
llllllllllllll!!!!!!!!!!!!!!!!!!!*

The Leicester fans carried on booing him, but David was back to being a Manchester United hero.

'Love him or hate him, you can't keep a great player down!' the TV commentator yelled over the Old Trafford noise.

David felt a wave of relief rush through his body. After his moment of madness at the World Cup, he had thought about leaving his childhood club and moving to Spain or Italy.

'Stay!' Keano had told him. 'We need you!'

David could never say no to his scary captain. He wasn't going anywhere, not yet. He couldn't just run away from trouble. There was more that he wanted to win at Manchester United. First of all, they needed to take the Premier League title back from Arsenal. After that, who knew? United had won The Double in 1997, so why not The Treble in 1999? David always set himself ambitious targets.

After a slow start to the season, United stormed ahead of Arsenal. Their team spirit was unbreakable, thanks to their amazing manager.

'It's never over until that final whistle blows!'
Fergie reminded them again and again.

The players always believed they would win and
whenever it looked like they might lose, someone
saved the day.

There were so many matchwinners in the team –
Giggsy, Scholesy, Dwight Yorke, Andy Cole, Teddy
Sheringham and super sub Ole Gunnar Solskjær.
Nicky got the key goal against Leeds United and even
Gary got on the scoresheet against Everton.

A lot of the time, David was the one who set
up the goals with his incredible crosses, free kicks
and long-range passes. But in the final weeks of the
season, he put his shooting boots on. With Arsenal in
second place breathing down Manchester United's
necks, his team needed him.

United were losing 1–0 at Wimbledon with seconds
left in the first half. David crossed towards Andy, but
he couldn't quite reach it. As the ball bounced around
in the box, David sprinted bravely forward to score.

Goooooooooooooaaaaaaaaaallllllllllllllllllllll!!!!!!!!!!!!

It was one of his scrappiest strikes, but it was also one of his most important.

'Yes, Becks!' Dwight cheered, jumping on David's back.

United were drawing 1–1 with Aston Villa when they won a free kick. David stepped up and fooled the keeper by taking a long run-up. It looked like he was going for lots of power but, instead, he chipped the ball straight into the top corner.

Gooooooooooooooooooooaaaaaaaaaaaaaaaaaalllllllllllll llllllllllllll!!!!!!!!!!!!!!!!!!!!

David punched the air as he ran past the fans. 'The title is ours!' he shouted at the top of his lungs.

But on the final day of the season, United still needed to beat Tottenham to make sure. With the pressure on, they had to hold their nerve.

After twenty-five minutes, Tottenham were winning 1–0. The fans fell silent in the stands, but the players didn't panic. How many times had they fought back to win?

'Come on, we can do this!' Keano called out.

David charged around the pitch but when he got

a glorious chance to score, he fluffed it. His header flew over the bar from six yards out.

'Nooooooooo!' David cried out, putting his hands on his head.

What a miss. He had to be more composed than that.

At the end of the first half, he got a second chance. Giggsy passed to Scholesy, who passed to David. He was in space on the right, just inside the penalty area. He could cross to Dwight and Andy, but the shot looked like the better option.

'Stay calm,' David told himself. He took a touch to steady himself, then threw that left arm back and curled the ball towards the top corner. The goalkeeper got his fingertip to it, but he couldn't save it.

Goooooooooooooooooooaaaaaaaaaaaaaaaalllllllllll lllllllllllll!!!!!!!!!!!!!!!!!!

David leapt into the air, clenching his fists at the crowd. There was no smile on his face. He was fully focused on winning.

Early in the second half, Gary played a great long-ball through to Andy Cole, who lobbed the keeper. 2–1!

Finally, David allowed himself to smile as the

whole United team celebrated together. What a moment – they were so nearly there. Eventually, the final whistle blew.

Campeones, Campeones, Olé! Olé! Olé!

United! United! United!

The players celebrated their fantastic achievement together, but they couldn't party for long. Although the Premier League season was over, *their* season wasn't. United still had two big finals to play. The Treble was on.

In a bruising FA Cup semi-final in April 1999, they had faced Arsenal. It was still 0–0 after 120 minutes of football, so the tie went to a replay. It was the last thing United needed, but in the replay at Villa Park, David gave them the lead with another brilliant long-range strike. It was his eighth goal of the season and his new favourite.

But Dennis Bergkamp made it 1–1 and the game went to extra time again. Thankfully, Giggsy saved them from a horrible penalty shoot-out. He got the ball in his own half, dribbled through the whole Arsenal defence and scored.

Despite his tired legs, David chased after his team-mate. 'Giggsy, that's the greatest goal ever!' he roared.

After the full-time whistle, the fans stormed the pitch and lifted their two wing wizards up into the air.

'The final should be a piece of cake after that!' Giggsy joked.

It wasn't, but they made sure that they got the job done and beat Newcastle 2–0. Scholesy was their Wembley hero, with an assist for Teddy and then a goal of his own. Afterwards, David and his teammates formed a big circle on the pitch and danced up and down together.

Campeones, Campeones, Olé! Olé! Olé!
United! United! United!

Their season *still* wasn't over, though, and they could *still* win The Treble. In the Champions League Final, United faced Bayern Munich. This was the trophy that David wanted most because it was the biggest club trophy in the world, and Manchester United hadn't won it since 1968.

'This is our time!' Fergie told his players before the game. 'You've done so well to get this far, but let's finish off this season in style tonight!'

David had played in lots of big matches in lots of stadiums, but nothing compared to this. Barcelona's Nou Camp was packed with 90,000 supporters and the noise was deafening. David took a deep breath and closed his eyes. He had made it to the very top of world football.

'We *can't* let the fans down!' he told Giggsy before kick-off.

They were United's key players, especially as Keano and Scholesy were both suspended. They weren't, however, in their normal positions. Giggsy was now on the right wing and David was in the middle with Nicky. David had played there before but never in a game like this – the Champions League Final.

'You can do this!' Fergie told him, looking him straight in the eyes.

But after only six minutes, United were 1–0 down. What a shocking start! Where was Keano when they needed their leader?

'Heads up, lads!' Peter Schmeichel screamed, clapping his goalkeeper gloves together. He was their captain now. 'We've got plenty of time to score!'

United were the masters of the comeback. They had done it so many times already that season, including in the semi-final against Juventus. Could they do it one more time?

David tried to curl in as many crosses as possible, but it wasn't so easy from central midfield. With time running out, corners were their best route to goal. The team was relying on David to deliver yet again.

Three added minutes. Can United score? They always score!

Even Peter was up in the box, so David had to get it right. His corner was cleared, but only as far as Giggsy. He volleyed the ball towards goal and Teddy steered it in. 1–1!

As Teddy raced away to celebrate, David jumped on his back. The noise around the Nou Camp grew even louder. The Manchester United fans had never stopped believing and neither had the players.

'We can win this now!' Giggsy shouted.

United won another corner. As David sprinted over to take it, he was buzzing with confidence. His delivery was perfect, right in the danger zone. Teddy headed the ball towards goal and Ole stuck out a leg to poke it in. 2–1!

As the Bayern players sank to their knees in despair, David jumped for joy. It was the best feeling that he had ever felt. The subs all ran over to join in the celebrations, while Peter did cartwheels around his penalty area.

It was the most amazing end to a Champions League final ever. In less than three minutes, they had gone from losing to winning. It really was the perfect end to a perfect season. Manchester United had won the Treble, capping the most successful season in the history of the football club.

'We did it!' David cheered with one arm around Gary and the other around Giggsy.

He didn't want to let go of them. They were his brothers, his best friends and his teammates. And not only were they the Champions of England, but they were now the Champions of Europe too.

Campeones, Campeones, Olé! Olé! Olé!
United! United! United!

CHAPTER 14

EURO 2000

Playing for Manchester United, David was a fans' favourite, especially now that he had helped the club to win the Treble.

Playing for England, however, in 2000, David was still Enemy Number One. The fans hadn't forgiven him for his moment of madness against Argentina at the World Cup.

'That was two years ago!' he moaned to Gary. 'Isn't it time they moved on?'

His friend laughed. 'Maybe if you do something special, they will!'

As soon as his suspension ended, David had jumped straight back into the England team. He had helped his country to qualify for Euro 2000, but he still hadn't added to that free-kick goal against Colombia at the 1998 World Cup. Gary was right – he had work to do in order to make things right.

'You mean the haircut wasn't enough?' David kidded back. His famous blonde locks were gone. With a shaved head, 'the new Becks' meant business.

Hopefully, Euro 2000 would be his time to shine. There was a relaxed atmosphere around the England training camp, and everyone was excited about the tournament ahead. Kevin Keegan was the new manager but most of the players were still the same – Tony and Sol at the back, Incey and Scholesy in the middle, Alan and Michael up front. David was the first choice on the right wing, with Steve McManaman on the left.

'How's it going at Real Madrid, Macca?' David asked Steve. He liked the idea of playing in Spain one day.

'I'm loving it!' Steve replied. 'Didn't you see my goal in the Champions League final?'

It was England's best squad for years, but it needed to be. They were up against Portugal, Germany and Romania.

'Welcome to the Group of Death, lads!' Incey joked.

It wasn't going to be easy, but England got off to a brilliant start against Portugal. In the third minute, David curled the ball in from the right and Scholesy had a free header. 1–0!

'What a cross!' Scholesy cheered, jumping into David's arms. The members of Manchester United's Class of '92 had been playing together for so long that they knew each other's movements off by heart.

Fifteen minutes later, David burst down the right wing again. This time, he chipped the ball over Scholesy's head to Steve at the back-post. 2–0!

'I've got two assists already – is that special enough yet?' he grinned at Gary.

The answer was no. The fans continued to shout horrible abuse at David.

Unfortunately, it all went downhill after that for England. Michael and Macca got injured and Luís Figo and Rui Costa led Portugal to a Manchester

United-style comeback. By half-time, it was 2–2 and by full-time, England had lost 3–2. David was devastated but he shook hands and swapped shirts with Luís.

'Well played today,' the Portuguese player said. 'I thought my right foot was dangerous but yours is *deadly*!'

Luís's kind words made David feel a little better, but it was still a bad defeat for England.

'If we don't beat Germany, that's it,' David told Victoria anxiously on the phone, 'we're out of the tournament.'

With the pressure on, however, England upped their game. Early in the second half, they won a free kick on the right.

'Take a quick one!' Gary shouted.

David shook his head. 'No, go away!'

Instead, he swung a brilliant free kick into the penalty area. The ball flew past Michael, then Scholesy, but as it bounced down, Alan was there with a diving header. 1–0!

'Great cross!' Gary cried out as he hugged David.

'Surely they'll forgive you now!'

At the final whistle, David threw his arms up in the air. What a result! England had beaten Germany in a competitive match for the first time since 1966. It was the victory that they needed, and it was all thanks, once again, to his remarkable right foot.

A draw against Romania would be enough to send them through to the quarter-finals. At half-time, England weren't drawing; they were winning! They were 2–1 up, thanks to Alan and Michael.

'You just need to keep your heads now, boys,' Keegan told them in the dressing room. 'No silly mistakes!'

Unfortunately, just after the break, England did make a silly mistake and Romania scored. Watching the ball hit the net, David's shoulders slumped. Scholesy looked over at him and his face said it all – 'Uh-oh, we're in trouble!'

England held on, however, and with seconds to go, it looked like they were through. Romania launched one last attack. As Viorel Moldovan dribbled into the penalty area, it didn't look too dangerous. They had plenty of defenders in the box, and yet Phil decided to slide in for the tackle. Instead of the ball, he kicked Moldovan's leg. Penalty!

Near the halfway line, David watched in horror and disbelief. He put his hand to his head. It was another moment of madness in a major tournament. Romania scored from the spot, and England were out of Euro 2000. What a crushing blow.

If anyone would know how Phil was feeling, it was David. He went over and put an arm around his friend. 'Hey, that wasn't your fault, okay? We weren't good enough – all of us. It's as simple as that.'

After a few days of sulking, it was time for England to move on. When one international tournament ended, another began. They now had the 2002 World Cup to qualify for.

CHAPTER 15

CAPTAIN TO THE RESCUE

6 October 2001 – Old Trafford, Manchester
The fourth official stepped forward and lifted the electronic board above his head for everyone to see – '4'.

The noise level lifted around Old Trafford. There was still time! England had four more minutes to score. David chased after every ball, desperate to save his country from an embarrassing defeat. It was like he had endless amounts of energy. Playing for England meant so much to David and, after his red card in 1998, he *had* to play at the 2002 World Cup.

His tenth match as England captain really wasn't going according to plan. All they needed was a draw against Greece to finish top of UEFA Group 9, but instead, they were losing 2–1. It was like the Romania match at Euro 2000 all over again.

'Keep going!' David shouted, urging his teammates up the field.

Everything had been going so well, ever since Peter Taylor had given him the captain's armband in November 2000. Leading his country for the first time against Italy was the proudest moment of David's life. It made him feel even more determined out on the pitch. The whole nation was relying on him.

When Sven-Göran Eriksson arrived as the new England manager, he asked David to keep wearing the armband. 'Yes, please!' he said, and the Three Lions beat Spain 3–0, then Mexico 4–0 and, best of all, Germany 5–1.

He would never forget that amazing night in Munich. From 1–0 down, England fought back brilliantly. David helped to set up three of the goals, working brilliantly with Scholesy, Michael and Steven Gerrard.

That feeling of joy and success now felt like a lifetime ago. How could England thrash Germany and yet still not qualify for the World Cup? It seemed impossible.

Nigel Martyn kicked the ball downfield to Teddy. As he jumped for the header, the Greece defender pushed him in the back. A free kick in the ninety-third minute!

The noise level lifted around Old Trafford once more. This would be David's sixth free kick of the game, and his strikes were getting closer and closer. The last one had whistled just wide of the post. Could he do better with his final attempt?

David took his time, placing the ball down carefully. He wanted to make sure that everything was perfect before he took the last kick of the match. Teddy tried to take it himself, but nothing was going to stop David.

'Trust me, I've got this,' he said firmly.

Teddy saw the focused look on his captain's face and walked away. Scholesy stood to his right in silence. He believed in his friend and teammate. He had seen David do it so many times before, especially there at his football home, Manchester United's 'Theatre of Dreams', Old Trafford.

In the stands, the fans could barely watch. Some feared the worst, but others still held out hope. If anyone could score a last-minute free kick, it was 'Becks'. The banging of a drum echoed around the stadium. Even David could hear it down on the pitch.

As he waited for the referee's whistle, David took long, deep breaths to calm his pounding heart. He needed to be as calm and composed as possible. He felt confident. 'I can do this,' he told himself. He had spent so many years practising free kicks, practising for massive moments like this.

David looked up at the goal and imagined the ball flying into the top corner of the net. He imagined the celebrations up and down the country, and the newspaper headlines – 'DAVID BECKHAM: ENGLAND HERO'. Yes, he liked the sound of that. With one kick, he could at last put his 1998 World Cup nightmare behind him.

Finally, the whistle sounded. David moved towards

the ball, slowly at first but then faster. Everyone knew his technique. He swung his left arm backwards and his remarkable right foot forwards. Bang!

The ball curled up over the wall…

'I definitely hit that well,' David thought to himself as he stood and watched. He had a good feeling about this one.

… then dipped…

'He's done it!' the fans yelled, rising to their feet. 'He's done it!'

…and landed in the top corner of the net.

Gooooooooooooooooooooaaaaaaaaaaaaaaaaalllllllllllll llllllllllllll!!!!!!!!!!!!!!!!!!!

Captain to the rescue - David *had* done it! In that moment, the adrenaline took over. It felt even better than that Wimbledon Wonderstrike. He raced over to the fans in the corner and leapt into the air. As he landed on both feet, he threw his arms out in the air.

'We're off to the World Cup!' Emile Heskey shouted, giving him a big bear hug.

'Becks, you're a legend!' Rio Ferdinand screamed in his face.

Gary gave David the biggest hug of all. 'You know I said that you needed to do something special to win over the fans? That was it, mate! That was it!'

The dark days were over. All was forgiven.

Finally, he was back to being 'DAVID BECKHAM: ENGLAND HERO'.

CHAPTER 16

WORLD CUP 2002

With the 2002 World Cup only eight weeks away,
England's captain, David was in fine form for his
club. Manchester United were on their way to
another Premier League title and they were through
to the quarter-finals of the Champions League too.

Against Deportivo La Coruña, David got the
opening goal. It was his sixteenth of the season
already, and another long-range wonderstrike. That
remarkable right foot of his was simply unstoppable.

'What's going on?' Scholesy said as they celebrated.
'You're scoring more than me these days!'

Sadly, David's club season was about to end. In
the last minute of the game, Deportivo's striker
Diego Tristán caught him on the left foot with a bad

tackle.

'Argghhhh!' David cried out.

Even though he was in so much pain, his first worry was, 'What about the World Cup?'

David needed crutches just to leave the stadium. The England fans held their breath but a week later, he was back playing against Deportivo in the second leg.

'Just see how you get on,' Ferguson told him. 'If it starts to hurt, I'll bring you off.'

It all seemed fine for the first twenty minutes, but then Aldo Duscher slid in and sent David flying. It was another reckless challenge on his left foot and this time, the pain was ten times worse.

'Argghhhh!' David cried out again, rolling around in agony.

Eventually, the team physio helped him back to his feet, but it hurt just to stand. That's when David knew that something was seriously wrong.

'It's broken, isn't it?' he asked.

The physio nodded glumly. 'I think so.'

David's heart sank. There was no way that a

broken foot could heal in eight weeks. England would have to win the World Cup without him.

'Hey, you don't know that yet!' Victoria said in the ambulance on the way to the hospital. 'Let's just wait and see what the X-ray shows.'

David had never been so nervous in all his life. Finally, Victoria spoke to the doctors and brought him the news.

'Ok, so you *have* broken a bone in your foot called the metatarsal, but it looks like you should still be able to play at the World Cup,' she told him, a smile breaking out across her face.

'Really?' David replied. He was relieved but also surprised. How could a bone heal that quickly? He didn't want to get his hopes up for nothing.

'Yes, but the doctors say it's not going be easy. It sounds like a lot of hard, boring work.'

'No problem, I'll do anything I can to get fit in time!'

Day by day, the tournament got closer and closer. And day by day, David's left foot got better and better. The question on every English person's lips was: would 'Becks' be ready? The country's hopes seemed to rest on his metatarsal. It was a race against time, but like every football match he had ever played, he was determined to win.

'So, are you fit enough to play?' his manager Sven-Göran Eriksson asked a few days before the first game.

'Yes,' David replied, sounding certain. 'You try stopping me!'

With the whole nation cheering him on, he ran out as England captain against Sweden. David felt so proud to lead his country at a World Cup, especially after his injury problems. Once again, he had shown his strong character.

'Come on, boys!' he called out in the tunnel. 'Here we go!'

It was great to be back. After twenty-five minutes, David swung in one of his trademark corner-kicks and Sol powered the ball home with his head. 1–0!

Sadly, they couldn't hold on for victory. In the second-half, Niclas Alexandersson scored and the Three Lions had to settle for a draw. That put even more pressure on England's next game – the rematch against Argentina.

David wasn't the only one who wanted revenge after the World Cup of 1998; so did Sol, Scholesy, Michael, and an entire nation of football fans. But for David, revenge would be particularly sweet.

'Let's win this, lads!' he shouted confidently.

Both teams were really fired up, but England were on top. Just before half-time, Scholesy passed to Michael inside the box. As he tricked his way past Mauricio Pochettino, the defender stuck out a leg. Penalty!

Who would take it – Michael? No, David walked straight over and grabbed the ball. This was a goal that he needed to score. He placed it down on the spot and then stepped back, trying to keep his adrenaline under control.

As David looked up, his enemy, Diego Simeone, was walking towards him. He was trying to put David off, but it wasn't going to work. Just to make sure, Nicky and Scholesy pushed the Argentinian out of the way. They always had their friend's back.

With one last deep breath, David ran forward and… swept the ball past the keeper.

Gooooooooooooooooooooaaaaaaaaaaaaaaaaalllllllllllll llllllllllllllll!!!!!!!!!!!!!!!!!!!!

As he ran towards the fans, David lifted his shirt to his face and kissed the Three Lions.

'Come on!' he roared.

Four years of pain flashed before his eyes. He felt so emotional that he didn't know whether to laugh or cry. In the end, he did a bit of both.

That goal turned out to be the matchwinner. At the final whistle, the whole team ran over to hug David. He was definitely an England hero now.

The Three Lions roared on. With a 0–0 draw against Nigeria and a 3–0 over Denmark, they were through to the World Cup quarter-finals. Next up, Brazil and their '3 Rs' – Ronaldo, Rivaldo and Ronaldinho.

'Don't worry, Sol and I will handle those guys!' Rio reassured his teammates.

David's left foot had begun to hurt, and the warm weather in Japan wasn't helping his tired legs.

Still, the pain was all worth it to lead his country towards glory.

After twenty-three minutes, Michael gave England the lead. The team was really starting to believe that they could go all the way.

Rio and Sol kept Ronaldo quiet, but that still left Rivaldo and Ronaldinho. They scored the goals that took Brazil into the semi-finals.

David was very disappointed to get knocked out, but he was also proud of his team. England had done so well to get through 'The Group of Death' and reach the quarter-finals. David was also proud of himself. Not only had he recovered from injury just in time, but he had also redeemed himself against Argentina.

The England team's future looked bright. David couldn't wait for his next international adventures – Euro 2004 and then the 2006 World Cup.

CHAPTER 17

LEAVING OLD TRAFFORD

David returned to Manchester United, feeling as excited as ever about winning trophies. Even after five Premier League titles, two FA Cups and one Champions League trophy, he still wanted more.

David still had that incredible hunger that Alex Ferguson had spotted so many years ago. The Manchester United manager wasn't quite so sure, however. He noticed that David's dyed blonde hair was back, and that he had so many celebrity commitments. Was David *really* focused on football? Fergie pushed his players very hard. He expected 100 per cent effort from all of them, but especially from his 'Fledglings' like David.

'What more can I do to show him?' David asked

Gary. 'We're top of the Premier League and we're still in the Champions League!'

'Just keep playing well and everything will soon go back to normal,' his friend advised.

In the Champions League quarter-final, United were up against the 'Galácticos' of Real Madrid – Raúl, Roberto Carlos, Luís Figo, Zinedine Zidane and Ronaldo. It was already an amazing team but every summer, they signed a new superstar. Rumours were spreading that David would be next.

'No way!' he protested. 'I'm not going anywhere. I love it here in Manchester.'

In the first leg at Real Madrid's Bernabéu stadium, the Galácticos outplayed United. Luís got one goal and Raúl got two in a 3–1 win.

'Come on, we can still turn things around at Old Trafford,' David told his teammates on the way back to England.

United never gave up. They always believed that they could win, no matter what. That's what made them such a successful team – Gary, Phil, Keano, Nicky, David, Giggsy and Scholesy.

On the day of the second leg, however, Fergie called David into his office. 'I'm afraid that you're not starting tonight. You'll be on the bench.'

He couldn't believe it. Ahead of the biggest game of the season, he had been dropped. That hurt so much. David left Fergie's office without saying a word.

'That's it!' he muttered to himself as he stormed down the corridor.

For sixty minutes, David sat and watched Ronaldo tear United apart with an amazing hat-trick. It was awful to feel so helpless on the bench. David was itching to get out there and prove his manager wrong. Finally, he got his chance. United needed three goals – and quickly.

Straight away, David whipped in a brilliant cross for Ole Gunnar, but he headed just wide.

'Unlucky!' David clapped, urging his team to keep going.

United won a free kick just outside the Real Madrid penalty area. There was only one remarkable right foot that could take it, and there was only one place where the ball could end up. Bang!

Goooooooooooooooooooaaaaaaaaaaaaaaaallllllllllll llllllllllllll!!!!!!!!!!!!!!!!!!

David punched the air and high-fived Giggsy.
Only two more goals to go! In the middle of the
match, Roberto Carlos called out to him, 'So, are you
coming to play for us?'

David didn't reply. He was too busy trying to
keep United in the Champions League. Ruud van
Nistelrooy dribbled towards goal. His shot was saved
but David slid in to score his second of the night.

Goooooooooooooooooooaaaaaaaaaaaaaaaallllllllllll llllllllllllll!!!!!!!!!!!!!!!!!!

Only one more goal to go! In stoppage time,
United won another free kick just outside the Real
Madrid penalty area. Could David rescue his team
with a hat-trick? His strike flew over the wall,
towards the top corner... but just over the crossbar.

So close! United were out, but David felt proud of
his own performance. He had proved his dedication
to the club. As he walked around the pitch, the fans
gave him a standing ovation.

'Don't leave, Becks!' they shouted.

After that match, there were more and more stories about David moving to Real Madrid. It felt nice to be wanted by such a top club.

'It would be pretty cool to play with Zidane and Ronaldo...' he started thinking.

Out on the pitch, David finished the 2002–03 season in style. He scored against Charlton and Everton, as United sealed yet another league title. He was right at the heart of the team's celebrations, with one arm around Scholesy and the other around Juan Sebastián Verón.

'I love it here,' David thought to himself happily that day. 'No, I'm not going anywhere!'

In the end, however, it wasn't David's decision. During the summer, United accepted offers from Barcelona and Real Madrid.

David couldn't believe it. Was he really leaving Old Trafford after twelve incredible years? It was his home, the place where he had developed as a footballer and as a person. At Manchester United, his teammates weren't just teammates. Gary, Phil,

Nicky, Scholesy and Giggsy were his best friends, his brothers. David had grown up with them.

And what about his family? It was a huge decision for all of them. Could he make Victoria and their sons move to Spain? It would be a new life in a new country, with a new language and a new culture.

'We'll support you, whatever you choose to do,' his wife reassured him.

Well, if David was going to leave Manchester United, it could only be to join one club – Real Madrid. He loved playing at the Bernabéu, and he loved the stylish football that the Galácticos played. He spoke to their president on the phone.

'I think you are one of the best footballers in the world,' Florentino Pérez told him, 'and we believe that you can make our team even better.'

A few days later, the deal was done. David and his family were off on an exciting Spanish adventure. Before he could get down to football, however, he had to choose a shirt number. Raúl wore his favourite Number 7, Ronaldo wore Number 9 and Luís wore Number 10. What about 8 or 11?

'No, I'll take Number Twenty-Three,' David decided. That was the number that his basketball hero Michael Jordan had worn for the Chicago Bulls.

Dressed in a pale blue suit, David smiled for the cameras and held up the famous white Real Madrid shirt with '23 BECKHAM' on the back. He was now a Galáctico, playing for the Spanish champions. It was yet another dream come true.

'Hala Madrid!' David cheered.

CHAPTER 18

LIFE AS A GALÁCTICO

As David prepared for his first training session at Real Madrid, he couldn't help missing Manchester United. His life had been so easy there, playing with the same familiar players and managed by the same familiar manager.

Now, everything was different and daunting. He was about to meet his new teammates and what if they didn't like him? What if he didn't fit in?

David arrived early and sat in the dressing room, waiting nervously. He didn't want to steal anyone's seat, so he sat on the physio's bed instead.

Luís was the first to arrive.

'Hola, how are you?' he asked, with a friendly smile.

David's Spanish was poor, and his Portuguese was even worse, so he was relieved to hear Luis' excellent English.

The Galácticos entered one by one, each giving him a warm welcome.

'I knew you'd be here soon!' Roberto Carlos laughed.

'As soon as Macca leaves, another Englishman arrives!' Zinedine joked.

'Here you go,' Raúl smiled, handing David two sheets of paper. 'Your survival kit!'

It was a list of Spanish football phrases. 'Thanks, you're a lifesaver!' David replied.

David couldn't wait to get started at Real Madrid. It was an amazing opportunity and a real challenge too. Off the pitch, the Galácticos were a relaxed bunch but on it, they were hard-working professionals. David had lots to learn to earn his place amongst them.

The season started with the Spanish Super Cup Final against Mallorca. After a 2–1 away defeat, Real needed a big win in David's home debut. In front of the roaring Bernabéu crowd, the superstars came alive.

Roberto Carlos crossed to Raúl. 1–0!

Luís passed to Ronaldo. 2–0!

David celebrated both goals with his teammates, but he was desperate to get in on the act. He needed a goal or an assist. He struck a fierce free kick, but it curled just over the crossbar.

'Unlucky!' Roberto Carlos said, giving him a high-five. 'Keep going!'

In the second half, Ronaldo won the ball on the left wing. As he looked up, he spotted David in space in the middle. His cross was perfect. As the goalkeeper rushed out towards him, David kept his eyes on the ball and headed it calmly into the empty net.

Goooooooooooooooooooooaaaaaaaaaaaaaaaaalllllllllllll llllllllllllll!!!!!!!!!!!!!!!!!!!!

David jumped up and punched the air. He was off the mark in a Real Madrid shirt! As he raised his arms up, the fans cheered. He was officially a Galáctico now.

'Thanks mate!' David shouted to Ronaldo as they hugged.

His La Liga debut was even better. After two minutes, Ronaldo played a one-two with Raúl and then crossed to the back post. David raced in from the right wing to smash the ball into the net.

Goooooooooooooooooooaaaaaaaaaaaaaaaaallllllllllll lllllllllllll!!!!!!!!!!!!!!!!!!!!

This time, he jumped into Ronaldo's arms. 'You're the best!' he cheered.

All that was missing now was one of David's famous free kicks. The fans were desperate to see one. Against Málaga, Roberto Carlos stood ready to run up and strike it but at the last moment, he moved away. It was David's turn! The goalkeeper moved to his left, but David put so much curl on the shot that it ended up in the opposite corner.

Goooooooooooooooooooaaaaaaaaaaaaaaaaallllllllllll lllllllllllll!!!!!!!!!!!!!!!!!!!!

Even David was surprised by how quickly he had settled in at Real Madrid. After only a month, he was already a key part of the team. With so many superstars on the pitch together, someone had to track back and help the defence. David was happy to be that someone. He had the energy and work rate to get up and down the pitch all game long.

'Finally, a Galáctico who doesn't just attack, attack, attack!' their goalkeeper Iker Casillas joked.

David still had that remarkable right foot, though. At times, it was like a magic wand.

Against Valladolid, he played a spectacular long pass from right to left for Zinedine to volley into the net. 4–0!

Against local rivals Atlético Madrid, he played an even more spectacular long pass for Raúl to head the ball over the goalkeeper. 2–0!

Everything was going so well. By March, Real Madrid were top of the Spanish league and into the Spanish Cup final. David couldn't wait to win more trophies.

In the final against Real Zaragoza, he scored another incredible free kick to give his team the lead. But just as the supporters got ready to party, their team collapsed in spectacular style; Real Madrid lost 3–2 in extra time.

'How did we let that happen?' David groaned, staring down at the grass beneath his feet. He hated losing so much, especially in finals.

It was a huge blow for the Galácticos and things soon got even worse. Back in the league, they lost six out of their last seven matches and ended up down in fourth place.

The fans were furious. With so much talent in the team, why weren't Real Madrid winning everything?

'Get ready for some changes this summer,' Roberto Carlos warned David.

During his twelve years at Manchester United, David had only ever played under one manager – Fergie. He was always there, and everyone trusted him.

At Real Madrid, however, they fired managers all the time. There was so much pressure to be successful straight away. During the 2004–05 season alone, David had three different bosses.

'This is ridiculous!' he complained to Michael

Owen, who had just joined him in Madrid. 'How are we supposed to win things with all this chaos around us?'

For the next two seasons in a row, Real Madrid finished second behind Barcelona. It was very frustrating to get so close to the title, and to lose out to their biggest rivals. Sometimes, the Galácticos were unstoppable but sometimes, they fell apart.

David, however, refused to give up. As Fergie had always taught him, it wasn't over until the final whistle blew. After winning so many trophies in England, David couldn't leave Spain empty-handed.

'I won't stop until we win the league!' he promised his teammates.

CHAPTER 19

PORTUGAL PAIN
PART I

David had a good feeling about Euro 2004. Looking around at all the talent in the squad, he truly believed that he could be the England captain who would finally end the thirty-eight years of hurt since 1966. How amazing would that be!

The Golden Generation was at its peak. In defence, Gary and Sol were joined by John Terry and Ashley Cole. In midfield, David and Scholesy were joined by Steven Gerrard and Frank Lampard. And in attack, Michael was joined by an eighteen-year-old wonderkid called Wayne Rooney.

'This is our best chance yet!' David kept telling his teammates. 'We just have to believe!'

That was especially important in the first match

against Zinedine's France, the winners of Euro 2000.

As he led the team out onto the pitch in Portugal, David could see the calm confidence on everyone's faces. They could beat France; they could beat anyone!

Late in the first half, England won a free kick on the right. David was ready to take it with his remarkable right foot. The ball fizzed in towards Frank and he glanced it into the top corner. 1–0!

'Get in!' David roared, punching the air.

In the second half, he played a great pass upfield to Wayne, who dribbled all the way into the box before a defender hacked him down. Penalty!

Once more, David was ready to take it with his remarkable right foot. England wouldn't get a better chance to go 2–0 up. He just had to beat his old Manchester teammate, Fabien Barthez.

David struck the ball well and right towards the corner but Barthez had guessed the right way. He flung himself across the goal. Saved!

Never mind, there was no time for David to feel sorry for himself. He chased back to defend, calling out, 'Come on boys, we're still 1–0 up!'

England held on bravely until the ninetieth minute when France won a free kick and Zinedine stepped up to take it. David jumped up in the wall, but the ball curved round them and into the bottom corner. 1–1! Zinedine's was a strike that even he would be proud of.

'Never mind, lads,' David shouted, trying to lift the spirits around him. 'A draw will do – focus!'

But in the final seconds, Steven played a back pass without looking behind him. Thierry Henry was on to it in a flash and he got to the ball just before the sliding goalkeeper. Penalty! Zinedine sent David James the wrong way, and it was 2–1 to France!

The England players stood there in shock. How had they lost that? David couldn't stop thinking about his spot-kick miss. If it had gone in, they would have won for sure.

'No mate, that wasn't a bad penalty,' Scholesy told him. 'It was a great save.'

It was time to move on. David was the captain and he had to make his teammates believe again.

'For ninety minutes, we were brilliant,' he told

them. 'If we keep playing like that, we'll win our next two matches. Forget about those last three minutes – we're better than that!'

England went on to beat Switzerland and Croatia in style, with Wayne scoring four goals. The team was in great form, so why couldn't they go all the way and win Euro 2004?

'Let's take one game at a time,' Gary warned from experience. 'This is knockout football now – any mistakes will cost us big time.'

Those were wise words, especially as England were about to play the hosts of the tournament in the quarter-finals. As well as having the home crowd behind them, Portugal also had lots of dangerous attackers, like David's Real Madrid teammate, Luís Figo, and his replacement at Manchester United, Cristiano Ronaldo.

None of that fazed England, though. Michael scored in only the third minute of the match. What a perfect start!

'Right, focus!' Gary called out from the back.

The Three Lions battled brilliantly, even when Wayne limped off with an injury. The semi-finals were in touching distance.

'Last push now, lads!' David shouted, shaking out his tired legs. 'Keep going!'

But with ten minutes to go, Hélder Postiga scored to make it 1–1. After thirty minutes of extra-time, that became 2–2. It was time for penalties.

To atone for his infamous absence from the penalty shootout against Argentina at the World Cup in 1998, David went first for England. As captain, he had to stand up and take responsibility.

'I've got this,' he told his manager confidently.

As David placed the ball down on the spot, he felt sure that he would score. But as he ran up to kick it, his left foot slipped on the grass. He was off balance and his right foot sliced the shot horribly. The ball sailed high over the crossbar.

'Nooooooooo!' David screamed, staring down at the pitch for answers. What had just happened? Why wasn't the ball in the back of the net? His remarkable right foot had failed.

David's heart sank. He had worked so hard to turn things around for his country, from villain in 1998 to hero in 2002. Now, he was England's villain once more.

Before Michael took the next penalty, he stamped down the turf around the spot. England couldn't afford to miss another one. Thankfully, he scored, and so did Frank, and so did John Terry, Owen Hargreaves and Ashley Cole. The shoot-out went to sudden death.

On the halfway line, David could hardly watch as Darius Vassell made the long walk forward. The Portugal goalkeeper, Ricardo, had taken his gloves off. He was *that* confident that he was going to save Darius' penalty, and he did. Ricardo then took Portugal's winning penalty himself.

David was devastated but he didn't forget his captain's role. Just as he had with Phil at Euro 2000, he went over and put his arm around Darius.

'Hey, you did everything you could tonight. Be proud. We'll get another chance, I promise!'

David's international dreams now rested on the 2006 World Cup. England certainly had the talent to win it, but did they have the nerve? Only time would tell.

CHAPTER 20

PORTUGAL PAIN PART II

With two wins and a draw, England got off to a strong start at the 2006 World Cup in Germany, and qualified for the knockout stage. The team spirit was sky high in the squad. They were determined to stay strong and conquer, despite the injuries.

Just as Wayne returned, Michael was stretchered off. But fear not! With David delivering incredible crosses to 'Two Metre' Peter Crouch, the dream was still alive.

Next up was Ecuador. They weren't as famous as their South American rivals Brazil and Argentina, but they still had plenty of skill and speed. At half-time, England were lucky to still be level at 0–0.

'Come on lads, wake up!' David shouted in the
dressing room.

With Michael and Scholesy missing, he was now
their most experienced attacker, as well as their
captain. Wayne still wasn't 100 per cent fit, and
Steven and Frank were struggling to score. That left
David and his remarkable right foot. What could he do
to lead England to the World Cup quarter-finals again?

'What's going on with your free kicks, Becks?'
Wayne had been teasing him in training. 'They've
been rubbish so far! Are you losing your golden
touch?'

His first attempt flew harmlessly wide, but that
didn't get David down. He just hoped that he would
get a second chance. When it arrived, he knew
exactly what he had to do.

As he waited for the whistle, lots of England
memories flooded through his head:

The free kick against Colombia at the 1998 World
Cup, his first ever international goal.

The free kick against Greece to save the day for his
country.

The successful penalty against Argentina at the 2002 World Cup.

The missed penalties against France and Portugal at Euro 2004.

But what about the 2006 World Cup? David was determined to make it a happy memory for himself and for the millions of England fans watching.

From wide on the left, he had two options:

1) Curl a cross into the penalty area

2) Curl a shot into the top corner.

Option 1 was what everyone was expecting – the England players in the box, the England supporters in the stadium, and, most importantly, the Ecuador goalkeeper.

With that thought in his head, David went for Option 2 instead. He was desperate to score a goal for his country and he might not get a better chance.

'Get one for me today,' his Real Madrid teammate Roberto Carlos had texted him earlier that day.

The angle wasn't easy, but David's accuracy was amazing. The ball clipped the post on its way into the net.

*Goooooooooooooooooooooaaaaaaaaaaaaaaaaalllllllllllll
lllllllllllllll!!!!!!!!!!!!!!!!!!!!!*

'YES!' David cried out as his teammates rushed over to him. What a crucial strike! He was now the first England player in history to score in three different World Cups.

'You've still got it, Becks!' Wayne cheered, looking mightily relieved.

In the crowd, Victoria jumped for joy. Her husband was the national hero once again.

England were through to the World Cup quarter-finals again, but they had to work to do. If they played that badly again against Portugal, Luís and Cristiano would hammer them.

'We've got to keep our heads,' David told the players, 'but let's show some passion out there. This is our chance for revenge!'

In the end, David only lasted fifty minutes in the harsh sun. After his heroics against Ecuador, he was struggling with illness and injury. He was desperate to carry on for his country, but his ankle was getting more and more painful.

'Good luck, go use your speed!' he told his replacement, Aaron Lennon.

From the bench, David watched another England moment of madness. Wayne was getting more and more frustrated with Portugal's tough tackling.

'Come on, ref!' he screamed. 'They're fouling me every time!

Wayne needed to calm down, but David wasn't there on the pitch to look after him anymore. After one more heavy challenge, the striker lost his temper. Red card!

'Here we go again,' David thought to himself. First Argentina, and now Portugal.

Again, England battled on bravely. Again, the match went to penalties, and again, England lost.

'We're cursed,' David muttered, with his head in his hands.

After a few minutes, he picked himself up and went back onto the pitch to thank the fans for all their support.

Was David saying goodbye? He wasn't sure, but he was sure about one thing:

'It has been an honour to captain my country for fifty-eight games, but I feel the time is right to pass on the armband,' he announced sadly.

Was that the end of David's World Cup dream? Not necessarily. At the next tournament in 2010, he would be thirty-five but if he was fit enough and his country needed him, he would never say no to England.

CHAPTER 21

OFF TO AMERICA

During the 2006–07 season at Real Madrid, David started thinking about his future. He wasn't playing as many games under new manager Fabio Capello, and his contract would soon run out. So, what next? At thirty-one years of age, David still had plenty of time left for one more football adventure.

'Where do you want to go?' his agent asked him. 'Back to England?'

David shook his head. He loved Manchester United too much to play for one of their Premier League rivals.

'Have you thought about America? Major League Soccer would love to have a player like you, especially at your age.'

In the past, fading superstars had often moved
to the USA for one final season. The American
fans loved to see famous faces but what they really
wanted was top players in their prime. David fitted
that description perfectly.

'You could help to change the image of the MLS
and turn it into a great league,' his agent continued.
'Who knows, maybe one day you could even have
your own club!'

David loved that idea. Los Angeles was one of his
favourite places in the world and their team, the LA
Galaxy, soon made him an offer that he couldn't
refuse.

'I guess a Galáctico has to join the Galaxy!' he
laughed.

At the end of the season, David would be off to
America. First, however, he put all of his effort into
winning the Spanish League with Real Madrid. He
fought his way back into the starting line-up and
set up lots of important goals. Finally, after years of
trying, Real Madrid beat their big rivals Barcelona to
the title.

Campeones, Campeones, Olé! Olé! Olé!

David was delighted with his winners' medal. It was the perfect way to end four fantastic years as a Galáctico.

'Adiós!' he waved to the amazing Real Madrid fans.

'Hello!' he waved to the people of America. They were very excited about his arrival. 'Becks' was going to take the MLS to the next level.

Back home, however, people criticised David's move:

'He's only going for the money. Why else would you go and play "soccer" out there?'

'Surely, that's the end of his England career? The MLS is rubbish!'

As always, David just ignored the cruel comments. They weren't true. He wasn't in LA for a beach holiday. He was fully focused on playing football and proving people wrong about American 'soccer'.

'And there's no reason why I can't keep representing my country!' he argued passionately.

David's first few seasons with the Galaxy weren't

as successful as he'd hoped. Despite scoring some trademark free-kicks and a Wimbledon-esque wonderstrike, he couldn't lead the team to MLS glory. He was selling lots of tickets and shirts, but he wasn't lifting trophies.

'It's great that more people are watching us,' he told his new manager Bruce Arena, 'but I want them to watch us *win*!'

With David's help, the Galaxy got better and better. In 2009, they lost to Real Salt Lake on penalties in the MLS Cup Final. It was a cruel way to lose but David stayed positive.

'Heads up, guys, we're getting closer!'

By 2011, they had one of the best attacks in the league. American star Landon Donovan and Irish star Robbie Keane were the strikers, with David creating magic in central midfield. The fans called them 'The LA Power Trio'.

In the quarter-finals of the MLS Cup, they faced Thierry Henry's New York Red Bulls. It was a battle of the former Premier League stars.

'It's like Manchester United vs Arsenal all over

again!' they joked before kick-off.

Once the match started, however, David was determined to come out on top. He set up all three goals with his remarkable right foot.

'Come on, this is our year!' he cheered confidently.

Thirty thousand fans filled the stadium in California to watch David and co take on the Houston Dynamo in the 2011 MLS Cup Final. After a frustrating first half, the Galaxy's stars came out to shine. David flicked a header on to Robbie, who passed through to Landon, who lifted his shot over the keeper. 1–0!

A smile of joy and relief spread across David's face. At the final whistle, Landon jumped into his arms.

'We've done it!' they screamed together.

After five years of trying, David had finally achieved his American Dream. He was an MLS champion. As he lifted the cup above his head, confetti filled the air and the crowd roared. David's sons Brooklyn, Romeo and Cruz joined him on the pitch, all wearing LA Galaxy scarves.

'Well done, Dad!' they cheered. It was a proud moment for the whole family.

David had only signed a five-year contract at the Galaxy, and those five years were now up. What next? He decided to stay in Los Angeles for another season.

'I want to win back-to-back MLS Cups!' David told the media.

And that's exactly what he did. For the 2012 final, the Galaxy were back at the same stadium against the same opponents, the Houston Dynamo. Would the LA Power Trio come out on top again?

David played a beautiful long ball to Robbie, who passed across to Landon in the penalty area, who... shot wide! All three of the Galaxy stars stood with their hands on their heads. They couldn't believe they weren't 1–0 up. By half-time, however, they were 1–0 *down*.

'Come on, we just need to take one of our chances,' David told his teammates.

He was desperate to be the Galaxy hero in his last game for the club, but in the end, it was Landon and

Robbie who scored the crucial goals. As long as his team won, David didn't mind.

'Back-to-back, baby!' Landon laughed.

After eighty-nine minutes, David was substituted and the fans all stood up to clap their superstar. When he first arrived in LA, he had promised them glory and he hadn't let them down.

David had left Real Madrid with a trophy and now he was leaving the LA Galaxy with a trophy too. It felt like the perfect way to end his American adventure. His final farewell, however, was even more perfect.

The US President invited the whole team to the White House for a special celebration. It was a huge honour.

'David, half of your teammates could be your kids,' Barack Obama joked during his speech. 'We're getting old, though you're holding up better than me!'

CHAPTER 22

MILAN AND PARIS

Even during his American adventure, David kept
in touch with Europe's top clubs. The MLS season
finished in December each year, so he needed to
keep himself fit during the break leading up to the
Spring.

'If I'm going to make the 2010 World Cup squad,'
David argued, 'I can't just sit around on the beach!'

In January 2009, he joined Italian giants AC Milan
on loan. It was an amazing opportunity to play with
lots of the best players in the world – Paolo Maldini,
Clarence Seedorf, Kaká, Andrea Pirlo, Andriy
Shevchenko, Ronaldinho... the list went on and on.

AC Milan were the 'Galácticos' of Italy, which

suited David perfectly. After his days at Real Madrid, he was used to playing in a team full of superstars.

'Don't worry, you just focus on your skills!' he joked with Ronaldinho. 'I'll do all the running for you!'

David wasn't as quick as he used to be, but in other ways, he had improved over the years. Rather than playing on the right wing, he often now played in central midfield. Experience had taught him to read the game well and spot the space before anyone else. He was a more intelligent footballer now.

Against Bologna, David got the ball on the right side of the penalty area. He faked to cross like normal but instead, he beat the keeper at his near post.

Goooooooooooooooooooooaaaaaaaaaaaaaaaalllllllllllll lllllllllllllll!!!!!!!!!!!!!!!!!!!

'Mate, that was clever!' Clarence shouted.

In the next match against Genoa, AC Milan won a free-kick wide on the left. 'I've got this one,' David told Andrea confidently. It was time to show that his remarkable right foot was still as deadly as ever. David faked to cross the ball into the box but again, he curled it in at the near post instead.

Goooooooooooooooooooooaaaaaaaaaaaaaaaallllllllllll llllllllllllll!!!!!!!!!!!!!!!!!!!

David hoped that the England manager, Fabio Capello, was watching. His AC Milan manager certainly was.

'You're making an enormous difference here!' Carlo Ancelotti said happily. 'How long can you stay?'

In the end, David stayed until the summer, and he returned the next year too. He loved Italian life and his top teammates. He even got to play at Old Trafford again, when AC Milan took on his beloved old club in the Champions League.

'Welcome home, Becks!' Scholesy said with a smile.

It was an incredible feeling to run on to his favourite pitch once more and hear the Manchester United fans chanting his name. At the end, David picked up a club scarf and wrapped it around his neck. He would always be a Red Devil at heart – and, of course, a proud Englishman. Sadly, however, David missed the 2010 World Cup through injury. That spelt the end of his international career.

Through the highs and the lows, it had always

been a pleasure and an honour to represent England. He had made 115 appearances for his country, 58 of those as the captain. He had played at three World Cups, scoring in each of them. A total of 17 goals in 14 years didn't sound like much, but each strike was so important, none more so than that free kick against Greece in 2001.

'We'll miss you,' the new national team captain, Steven Gerrard, told him. 'The World Cup won't be the same without you!'

David's club career wasn't quite over yet, though. After returning to the LA Galaxy and ending his American adventure in style, he accepted one last challenge at Paris Saint-Germain in France.

'Come to PSG, we need your experience!' his old AC Milan manager Ancelotti persuaded him.

When it came to football, David couldn't say no. It wasn't about the money at all. In fact, he donated all of his salary to children's charities. No, for David, it was all about his love for the beautiful game.

'Let's do this!' he said, feeling just as excited as when he played his first match for Manchester

United twenty years earlier.

When David arrived, PSG were already top of the table. Did they really need him? Yes! His new teammates welcomed him immediately, even star striker Zlatan Ibrahimović.

'Great, now that you're here, maybe the paparazzi will leave me in peace!' he joked.

David and Zlatan quickly became best mates, both on and off the pitch. With his amazing long passes and crosses, David helped to set up lots of goals for his Swedish friend.

'Are you sure you want to retire at the end of this season?' Zlatan asked as they hugged. 'We've got a great connection!'

It was very tempting to carry on at PSG, but David had already made his decision. After winning the league in England, Spain, the USA and now France, it was time to hang up his boots.

'I know I don't look it, Zlat, but I'm thirty-eight!'

Ancelotti made David captain for his final home game against Brest. It was a very emotional day with his family there watching. There was time for him to set up one last goal before he left the field for good. As he hugged his teammates one by one, the tears streamed down his face.

On the big screens, the message was short and sweet: 'THANK YOU, DAVID'.

In the stands, the PSG fans stood to clap and cheer their English star. He had only been at the club for five months, but he had left his mark.

David Beckham! David Beckham! David Beckham!

He was really going to miss that incredible feeling of love and support. Whether he was playing for Manchester United, England, Real Madrid, LA Galaxy, AC Milan or PSG, David had always given 100 per cent out on the pitch.

Even during the most difficult moments of his career – getting sent off against Argentina in 1998, leaving Old Trafford in 2003 – he had never given up. That's why fans around the world loved David. That, and of course, his remarkable right foot.

ENGLAND'S NEXT SUPERSTAR

2005

'Welcome!' David announced to a group of sixteen boys and girls. He was there in East London to launch his brand new football academy. 'Today, we're going to practise some of my favourite skills.'

With their hero watching and cameras everywhere, none of the kids wanted to make any silly mistakes as they dribbled up and down. One boy, however, was particularly eager to impress.

'That's it, great work everyone!' David called out.

At the end of the day, he shook each of them by the hand and chatted with them. When it was the boy's turn, he was too nervous to speak.

'Well done today. Are you one of the lads from Chingford?' David asked. He had invited a group from his old secondary school.

The boy nodded. 'A-and I play for Ridgeway Rovers too.'

David smiled. 'Great club. So what's next? What's your dream?'

'I want to play for England at Wembley!'

'Good choice, it's the best feeling in the world. If you keep working hard, you can do it. What's your name, kid? I'll have to remember you for the future!'

'Harry,' the boy replied, growing in confidence. 'Harry Kane.'

DAVID BECKHAM HONOURS

Manchester United

🏆 FA Youth Cup: 1992

🏆 Premier League: 1995–96, 1996–97, 1998–99, 1999–2000, 2000–01, 2002–03

🏆 FA Cup: 1995–96, 1998–99

🏆 UEFA Champions League: 1998–99

Real Madrid

🏆 Liga: 2006–07

🏆 LA Galaxy

🏆 MLS Cup: 2011, 2012

PSG

🏆 Ligue 1: 2012–13

Individual

🏆 PFA Young Player of the Year: 1996–97

🏆 Premier League PFA Team of the Year: 1996–97, 1997–98, 1998–99, 1999–2000

🏆 Premier League leader in assists: 1997–98, 1999–2000, 2000–01

🏆 UEFA Club Footballer of the Year: 1998–99

🏆 Ballon d'Or – Runner-up: 1999

🏆 UEFA Team of the Year: 2001, 2003

🏆 England Player of the Year: 2003

🏆 Real Madrid Player of the Year: 2005–06

🏆 MLS Comeback Player of the Year Award: 2011

BECKHAM

7, 23 32

THE FACTS

NAME: David Robert Joseph Beckham

DATE OF BIRTH: 2 May 1975

AGE: 44

PLACE OF BIRTH: Leytonstone

NATIONALITY: English

BEST FRIEND: Gary Neville

CURRENT CLUB: Manchester United, Real Madrid, LA Galaxy, AC Milan, PSG

POSITION: RM

THE STATS

Height (cm):	**183**
Club appearances:	**719**
Club goals:	**129**
Club trophies:	**18**
International appearances:	**115**
International goals:	**17**
International trophies:	**0**
Ballon d'Ors:	**0**

★ ★ ★ **HERO RATING: 89** ★ ★ ★

GREATEST MOMENTS

17 AUGUST 1996, WIMBLEDON 0-3 MANCHESTER UNITED

David was already a famous footballer in England, but this Wimbledon Wonderstrike turned him into an international superstar. In the first match of the Premier League season, David got the ball just inside his own half and decided to take a long-range shot. The incredible strike flew over the keeper's head and into the net. Even Eric Cantona said, 'What a goal!'

26 JUNE 1998, COLOMBIA 0-2 ENGLAND

Nearly two years after his England debut, David was still waiting for his first international goal. It finally arrived in the 1998 World Cup against Colombia and, of course, it was a trademark free-kick. David swung his left arm backwards and his remarkable right foot forwards. Bang! The ball flew into the bottom corner.

26 MAY 1999, MANCHESTER UNITED 2-1 BAYERN MUNICH

In the 1999 Champions League Final, Manchester United had the chance to win a historic Treble. With Roy Keane and Paul Scholes both suspended, David was under even more pressure to deliver. With three minutes to go, they were 1-0 down but thanks to two brilliant corner-kicks from David, United fought back to win 2-1. 'Fergie's Fledglings' just never gave up!

6 OCTOBER 2001, ENGLAND 2-2 GREECE

With seconds to go at Wembley, England were losing 2-1 and their World Cup 2002 dreams were in tatters. When they won a free-kick, David had one last chance to save the day for his country. He swung his left arm backwards and his remarkable right foot forwards. Bang! The ball flew into the top corner. Thanks to David, England were off to the World Cup.

10 APRIL 2005, REAL MADRID 4-2 BARCELONA

David enjoyed four very happy years as a Galáctico at Real Madrid. He managed to win the La Liga title, and this *El Clásico* win against big rivals Barcelona was probably his Spanish highlight. Although David didn't get on the scoresheet, he set up goals for Ronaldo and Michael Owen with his remarkable right foot.

PLAY LIKE YOUR HEROES

THE DAVID BECKHAM
FREE-KICK WINNER

STEP 1: Place the ball down, pick your spot, and take six steps back in a diagonal line.

STEP 2: As you run up, swing your left arm backwards and lean your shoulders back slightly. This will help you to lift the ball over the wall.

STEP 3: At the same time, swing your right foot forwards and strike the bottom of the ball with the side of your big toe. This will give you lots of extra curl to bend it like Beckham!

STEP 4: Plant your left leg to help you balance. Your toes should point towards where you want your free-kick to go.

STEP 5: Goal! Run towards the fans with your arms out wide like the hero you are. As you get close, leap up and punch the air.

STEP 6: Practice, practice, practice! Practice makes perfect.

TEST YOUR KNOWLEDGE

QUESTIONS

1. Which team does David's dad, Ted support?

2. Which team did David's grandad support?

3. What gift did David give to Sir Alex Ferguson when he was 13?

4. Name 3 other members of Manchester United's Class of 92?

5. Which England club did David join on loan in 1995?

6. Which England manager gave David his international debut?

7. Why did David choose the Number 23 shirt at Real Madrid?

8. Who were the other two members of the 'The LA Power Trio'?

9. Who was David's manager at both AC Milan and PSG?

10. How many World Cups did David go to with England?

11. How many World Cup goals did David score?

Answers below. . . No cheating!

1. Manchester United 2. Tottenham 3. A pen, which David later used to sign his first Manchester United contract. 4. Any of the following: Gary Neville, Phil Neville, Nicky Butt, Paul Scholes, Ryan Giggs, John O'Kane, Robbie Savage and Keith Gillespie. 5. Preston North End 6. Glenn Hoddle. 7. Raúl already had the Number 7 shirt and 23 was the number that his basketball hero, Michael Jordan, wore for the Chicago Bulls. 8. Landon Donovan and Robbie Keane 9. Carlo Ancelotti 10. 3 – 1998, 2002 and 2006 11. 3

GERRARD

TABLE OF CONTENTS

CHAPTER 1

ANFIELD FAREWELL

It was a sunny afternoon as the two teams walked out at Anfield, Liverpool in red and Crystal Palace in yellow. On the pitch, the players lined up opposite each other to form a tunnel. Liverpool only had ten – there was one very important player still to come.

'Ladies and gentlemen,' the announcer began. 'This club has been privileged to have many fantastic footballers putting on the red shirt over the years but this player, this man, is truly unique. Please raise your cards now to welcome your captain on to the pitch for his final game at Anfield, the one and only STEVIE GERRARD!'

Everyone in the stadium clapped and cheered as

Stevie walked on with his three daughters, Lilly-Ella, Lexie and Lourdes. As he moved down the line, the Crystal Palace players gave him high-fives. They had so much respect for all that Stevie had achieved.

Around the centre circle, Stevie waved to all of the fans who had helped to make his Liverpool career so special. He would never forget them, just as they would never forget him. In front of him, at the Kop end, was the most amazing thing he'd ever seen. There were lots of flags showing his name and face, and the fans were holding up cards that spelt out 'SG' in huge letters with the number '8' in the middle. Along the side of the pitch, the cards spelt out 'CAPTAIN'. The fans sang his chants again and again.

Steve Gerrard, Gerrard
He'll pass the ball forty yards
He shoots the ball really hard
Steve Gerrard, Gerrard

Stevie Gerrard is our captain
Stevie Gerrard is a red

Stevie Gerrard plays for Liverpool
A Scouser born and bred

Stevie had to fight back tears as he got ready for kick-off. The club meant so much to him but after seventeen seasons, it was time to leave Liverpool. He had touched the iconic 'This is Anfield' sign outside the dressing room for the last time as a Liverpool player and captain.

The Liverpool supporters sang 'You'll Never Walk Alone' at the top of their voices. Stevie would always get goosebumps when he heard the club anthem. The team was desperate to get a final win for Stevie and when Adam Lallana scored the opening goal, he ran to give Stevie a big hug. 'That was for you!' he said.

But Crystal Palace weren't interested in giving Stevie a happy ending to his Liverpool story. They scored two goals and suddenly Liverpool were risking defeat.

'I can be the hero one last time,' Stevie said to himself. 'I really want to score!'

He felt tired after another long season and every shot he took went wide of the goal. The fans called for him to keep shooting, but in the last minute Palace made it 3–1.

It was disappointing to end a club career with a defeat but it wasn't really about the result. It was about a captain saying goodbye to his supporters, and the supporters saying goodbye to their captain.

The Liverpool players came back out on to the pitch wearing '8 GERRARD' T-shirts.

'A whole team of Gerrards would be amazing!' Martin Škrtel joked with his teammates. 'We would definitely win the Premier League!'

As Stevie walked out, the singing started all over again. He waved to his wife, Alex, and his parents, Paul Sr and Julie, in the crowd. Without their love and strength, he couldn't have become such a superstar. The club presented him with a trophy in the shape of the Number '8' and then it was time for Stevie to speak. He had been dreading this moment for weeks. It was one thing scoring goals in front of 44,000 people but speaking was very different. He was very nervous but with Lourdes in his arms, he took the microphone.

'I am going to miss this so much,' he said, looking up into the stands. 'I'm devastated that I'll never play in front of these supporters again.'

Stevie thanked everyone at Liverpool: all of the coaches and managers he had played under, and all of the teammates that he had played with. He was so grateful to everyone for all of their support over the years.

'I've played in front of a lot of supporters around the world but you're the best,' he concluded. 'Thank you very much.'

It didn't feel real – was he really leaving Liverpool? When he was young, Stevie never thought that he would leave his beloved club. Top teams had tried to sign him but he had stayed loyal. It wasn't about money; it was about love and pride. Now he was off to play in the USA, for a new club in a new league – but nothing would ever compare to Liverpool.

He had played 709 games, 503 in the Premier League, and he had scored 119 goals. With his team, he had won the Champions League, the UEFA Cup, the FA Cup twice and the League Cup three times. He had so many amazing memories from his time at Anfield. It was here that he had grown up from a fierce-tackling skinny kid to become a world-class, goalscoring midfielder and the captain of club and country.

It had been an amazing journey for this young Liverpool fan from Huyton, and Stevie had loved every minute of it.

CHAPTER 2

HUYTON

'Paul! Stevie! Dinner!' Julie shouted from the front door of their house on Ironside Road. They lived in a nice community where everyone knew each other and the kids were free to play in the streets without any danger. The offer of food was usually enough to bring the children back home.

After waiting a minute, Julie heard the sound of running feet and saw her two sons turn the corner at the top of the road. Stevie was sprinting as fast as he could, with his little arms and legs moving very quickly. Behind him, Paul Jr was sprinting too. He was three years older than his brother and so it wasn't a very fair race.

Julie was so pleased that her sons were best friends. Of course, they had arguments sometimes but mostly, they couldn't be separated. Stevie wanted to do everything that his older brother did and Paul Jr wanted to look after his younger brother. The Gerrards were a very close, happy family. They didn't have lots of money, but there was always food in the cupboards and they always ate together.

Just as Stevie got near to their house, Paul Jr caught him.

'Got you!' he shouted as he grabbed his brother's shirt. Stevie slowed to a stop, panting hard. One day when he was a bit older and stronger, he would be able to outrun Paul Jr. But for now, he was just really hungry.

'What's for dinner, Mum?' he asked. Looking down at his trousers, he worried that he might be in trouble.

'Nothing until you two have a wash,' Julie replied. 'Paul, didn't I tell you to keep Stevie away from the mud? Look at you both – you're filthy!'

After a quick change of clothes, the family sat

down for a feast of burgers and chips. Paul Jr and Stevie wolfed the food down and asked for more. Their dad, Paul Sr, couldn't help but smile.

'I remember when I was a growing lad like you two. I could eat anything I wanted and I was still as thin as a rake. Now, look at me!' he said, patting his belly. His sons laughed and laughed.

'Stevie, take Granddad Sidney his tea and sit with him for a bit please,' Julie said once their meal was over. Her father was very ill and she looked after him in their house.

Stevie loved spending time with Granddad Sidney. He was a very kind man who loved his grandsons. Sidney had lots of great stories about Liverpool Football Club and his adventures with the British Navy. Stevie sat in a chair next to his bed and listened to him for hours.

'How's the football going?' Sidney asked.

'Paul's teaching me how to kick the ball really hard,' Stevie replied excitedly.

'Good, because I want a Liverpool player in this family,' Sidney said. He wasn't well enough to leave his bedroom but he watched lots of sport on TV. He often gave Julie money to buy his grandsons the latest Liverpool kit.

'Dad, you're spoiling them!' she told him, but it made him happy.

Stevie's other granddad, Granddad Tony, lived just down the street at 35 Ironside Road. Stevie loved having all of his family nearby. Some of his cousins and neighbours supported local rivals Everton instead of Liverpool and that made the derby matches really exciting. In the summer, all of the local families sat out in the street, eating and drinking and having a great time. The Bluebell Estate in Huyton was a great place to grow up.

After chatting to Granddad Sidney for a while, Stevie went looking for Paul Jr. His older brother had a bigger bedroom with a bigger bed and a bigger wardrobe. Stevie only had a tiny room but he didn't mind because Paul Jr was his hero.

The two spent a lot of time playing together, but sometimes, Paul Jr needed his own space. When he was hanging out with his friends, he didn't always want his younger brother around. One day, when he was sitting on a wall talking to a group of older boys, he pushed Stevie away, saying, 'Go home and find some mates!'

Any fights between Stevie and Paul Jr only ever lasted a few hours. Then they were best friends again. Every weekend, they sat on the sofa with their dad to watch *Match of the Day* on TV. When the theme music started, they all sang along. It was their favourite part of the week.

'That could have been me, kids,' their father said as they cheered a Peter Beardsley goal for Liverpool. Paul Sr had been a good footballer when he was young but he hurt his knee when he was fifteen. Now, he worked as a builder in the city, but he still encouraged his sons to excel at sport. 'And now, that can be you two!'

Julie didn't always watch the games but she was a Liverpool fan too – she didn't have any choice in such a football-mad family. If the boys weren't watching videos of old Liverpool victories, they were at Anfield watching Liverpool play live. Stevie loved standing on the Kop with his dad and brother. The atmosphere was amazing and the singing never stopped. It was extraordinary to watch players like Kenny Dalglish and John Barnes running down the Liverpool wing. The pitch looked so big and green, and Stevie was desperate to play there one day.

'Right, bedtime!' Julie would say when *Match of the Day* was over. Paul Jr and Stevie groaned but it was late and they could barely keep their eyes open. Slowly, they made their way upstairs.

'Paul, can we do more shooting tomorrow?' Stevie asked as he brushed his teeth. He would dream about the Beardsley goal for at least the next week.

'Sure – you'll be scoring great goals in no time!' his brother replied.

CHAPTER 3

HAPPY STREET

'Please let me come and play!' Stevie said to his brother as he rushed out of the front door with a football under his arm. Stevie was counting down the days until he could play his first match at 'Happy Street', the football pitch at the end of their road.

'How many times do I have to tell you? You're still too young,' Paul Jr told him. 'Some of the boys are really big and you'll get hurt.'

Stevie was six and his brother was nine but some of Paul Jr's friends were even older. They didn't want to play with a small, skinny kid who might cry if he fell over on the concrete. But Stevie wasn't scared;

he would do anything to make his debut at Happy Street.

'Please! I'll even go in goal if you want,' Stevie said. He wasn't giving up and his brother knew it.

'Fine, you can play but just don't embarrass me.'

'Yes!' Stevie shouted, jumping into the air. He was already in his lucky Liverpool shirt. He had been waiting for this moment for years. As they walked along the row of identical houses, Stevie thought about what he could do to impress the others. He needed to make sure that they let him play every day.

There were eight boys waiting for them by the goal and there were no cars in sight.

'Perfect – five-a-side,' Paul Jr said, taking a shot.

'Wait, Stevie isn't playing, is he?' their cousin Jon-Paul asked. 'He's tiny!'

'Yes he is but only for today and he says he'll play in goal,' Paul Jr replied. 'Don't worry about hurting him – he's my brother!'

He quickly picked the teams so that no-one else could complain, and made sure Stevie was on his team. Stevie stood between the goalposts and waited to make a save. The ball came flying towards him at great speed and he caught it bravely.

'Nice save, Stevie!' one of the boys shouted and Stevie's smile got even bigger.

Stevie was only wearing shorts but he was fearless. To stop goals, he dived to his right and he dived to his left. He had blood running down his knees but his team was winning thanks to a goal from Paul Jr. Suddenly, one of Stevie's teammates, Sammy, twisted his ankle.

'Are you alright?' Paul asked as Sammy sat on the floor in pain.

'No, I can't keep playing,' Sammy replied, trying to wiggle his ankle.

There was only one solution. 'Okay, do you think you could stand in goal?' Paul asked Sammy, helping him him back on his feet. Sammy nodded and limped towards the goal.

'Stevie, you're playing out on pitch now!' Paul shouted.

This was his big opportunity. Stevie rushed forward, he ran and ran and he made some good tackles but his teammates weren't passing to him. He was in lots of space on the right and his brother was dribbling towards goal.

'Paul! Pass to me!' Stevie shouted. At first, Paul Jr ignored him but then he saw that Stevie was the only free option. When he passed to him, he expected his little brother to lose the ball or take a weak shot. But Stevie controlled the ball and calmly looked up to see who he could pass to. Mark had made a run and Stevie played a perfect ball through the defence to him. Mark took one touch and scored.

Paul Jr jumped on Mark to celebrate but Mark ran over to Stevie. He gave him a big hug. 'What a pass, little man!' he shouted and Stevie felt on top of the world.

When he next got the ball, Stevie tried to dribble past one of the biggest boys but the boy pushed him to the floor. It really hurt his bleeding knees but Stevie was determined not to cry. He just had to get used to the hard tackles.

'Are you okay, Stevie?' Paul Jr asked, but his brother was already back on his feet and running into space. Paul Jr smiled; there was no stopping Stevie now that he was playing at Happy Street.

Jon-Paul scored two quick goals and suddenly it was 2–2. It was nearly dinner time and there were no streetlights at Happy Street when it got dark. Everyone was getting tired, except Stevie.

'Right, next goal wins!' Paul Jr shouted.

Stevie was desperate to be the hero. He chased the ball all around the pitch, trying to win tackles. He was like a bee buzzing around his opponents. They tried to swat him away but he wasn't giving up.

Paul Jr won the ball in defence and looked up. His teammates on the left and right were being marked closely. Stevie was their furthest player forward and suddenly he dashed into space. Paul Jr passed the ball and his little brother was through on goal. They had practised shooting in the back garden for hours and hours. Paul Jr hoped that Stevie would know what to do.

Stevie could hear a defender running towards him and he could see the goalkeeper in front of him. The goal looked so small – it seemed impossible to score.

If he waited too long, the defender would catch
up with him, or the goalkeeper would run out and
block him. It was time to shoot. Stevie aimed for the
bottom corner and pulled back his leg. He struck
the ball with as much power as his little legs could
manage.

The ball rocketed towards the goal. The keeper
dived but he couldn't quite reach it.

*Goooooooooooooooooaaaaaaaaaaaaaaaaaaaaaaaaaaa
aaaalllllllllllllllllllllllllllllllllll!!!!!*

Stevie couldn't believe it. Paul Jr and Mark lifted
him up into the air – he was the match-winner!

'What a finish, mate!' Sammy shouted as he
hobbled from the goal to join in the celebrations.

This was the best day of his life so far. Stevie
couldn't wait to tell the story to his dad. Paul Jr let
him proudly carry the match ball back to their house.

'Stevie's going to be a great player when he's
older,' Jon-Paul said.

Paul Jr nodded. 'Our family will have at least one
professional footballer!'

CHAPTER 4

MIDFIELD TERRIER

'John Barnes gets the ball on the left-wing, he dribbles past one defender and then another and then another! He's in the penalty area and he's just got the goalkeeper to beat... what a goal!' Stevie shouted as he kicked the ball into the net and then jumped into the air. He imagined that he was John Barnes playing for Liverpool and that his teammates like Ian Rush and Peter Beardsley were running over to congratulate him.

While he waited for the other boys to arrive for games at Happy Street, Stevie loved pretending to be his hero. Barnes was the most exciting player in the country, a really skilful midfielder who played for Liverpool and England. Stevie loved all of the Liverpool players but Barnes was the one he always wanted to be.

Stevie worked hard to improve his dribbling skills and his shooting but he wasn't a winger like Barnes. He was a midfield terrier who never stopped running from one great tackle to the next. If Stevie was around, no-one on the Bluebell Estate got more than a few seconds on the ball – and it was the same on the St Michael's school playground too.

Classes really got in the way of football, but break time and lunch time were awesome. Stevie took a packed lunch with him so that he could play for longer. He would take a few bites of a sandwich and then start kicking the ball. During lessons, he would write out the teams in the back of his exercise book so that everyone was ready to go.

'Right, you guys can kick off,' Stevie shouted.

The games were massive, hour-long battles. On a Sunday night, Julie laid out Stevie's clean school uniform but by Monday afternoon, it was already dirty. His smart shoes only ever lasted a few months.

'Sorry Mum!' he said when he got home from school. Julie was furious but eventually she had to relent – you couldn't stop Stevie from playing football. Even on a cold winter's evening nothing could stop the boys from playing on the estate, and Stevie would shiver in his shorts and Liverpool shirt.

One day, a car parked on Happy Street. A relative was visiting one of their neighbours and, of course, they weren't to know this concrete space was the 'pitch' where the boys played football. Stevie went straight up and knocked on his neighbour's front door.

'Hi, Stevie,' Mrs Fowler said as she opened the door. 'How can I help you?'

'Hi, Mrs F. Do you know anything about that car?' he asked, pointing towards the concrete space.

'Yes, that's my sister's car – she's on a day trip from Wales.'

'That's nice – could she move it, please?' Stevie asked.

'Oh,' Mrs Fowler replied. She was very surprised by Stevie's assertive request but he was smiling very politely. 'I don't know where else she can park...'

'I'm sorry, Mrs F, but that's our pitch!' Stevie interrupted.

Fifteen minutes later, the car was gone and the boys' game could finally begin.

Sometimes Stevie joined in games with his school friends but as fun as it was, the level was too easy for Stevie and so he preferred to challenge himself against his brother and his older friends. From Monday to Friday he played with them on the estate. At weekends, though, he was desperate to join them in their local Under-10s team, Tolgate. So one day, he went down to a training session there.

'Hello, can I join in please?' he asked the coach who was setting out the cones.

The coach looked at the small, skinny boy in front of him. 'How old are you, kid?' he asked.

Stevie thought about lying but he knew that his brother would tell the truth. 'Seven, but I play with older boys all the time, I promise.'

The coach shook his head. 'I'm sorry, lad, but you're just too young. Come back in a couple of years.'

On the walk home, tears streamed down Stevie's face. He kicked stones and coke cans as hard as he could. It wasn't fair; just because he wasn't the same age as the other boys didn't mean that he wasn't good enough. They should have given him a chance.

'I'll show them!' he said to no-one.

Stevie worked even harder on his touch and his toughness. He couldn't do much about his size or strength but being brave and fearless made a big difference. In one game on Happy Street, a twelve-year-old used his shoulder to push Stevie into the fence. His face scratched against a nail and he could taste the blood. But still Stevie didn't complain. He just ran across the road to Granddad Tony's house.

'Granddad, this won't stop bleeding,' he said and in ten minutes he was back out on the pitch with a big plaster on his face.

Paul was a good player but he didn't have the same determination as his younger brother. All Stevie wanted to do was become a top professional footballer like John Barnes, and finally, when he was eight, he took his first step towards Liverpool

Football Club: he joined a Sunday League team called Whiston Juniors.

'Great tackle, Stevie!' the manager, Ben McIntyre, shouted from the touchline.

It was only a training session but that didn't matter to this kid. He only ever played at 110 per cent and he had it all: not only pace and bravery but also skill and power.

'Okay, calm it down,' Ben told him. He needed to protect his star player from injury.

Stevie was the best player of his age that Ben had ever seen. The big question was how good could he become?

CHAPTER 5

SCOUTED BY LIVERPOOL

As a Liverpool youth coach and scout, Dave Shannon often got calls about exciting new football talent in the local area. He didn't have much spare time and so it was always difficult to work out which players were really worth watching. One night, Dave was relaxing at home when the phone rang. It was Ben McIntyre.

Straightaway Dave knew that this wasn't one of those normal phone conversations. Ben McIntyre was a good friend and the manager of Whiston Juniors. If he was calling about a young player then Dave trusted his advice.

'I've got this great kid that I think you should

really come and watch,' Ben said. 'We've got a game on Sunday if you're free?'

Dave could hear the excitement in Ben's voice. This youngster must be really good. 'If he's that good, just bring him to our training on Wednesday.'

'Sure, I'll do that,' Ben agreed.

'What's his name?' Dave asked, grabbing his notebook and a pen.

'Steven Gerrard.'

At the training session, at Vernon Sangster Sports Centre, Dave Shannon watched from the sidelines with his fellow coaches Hughie McAuley and Steve Heighway. The Under-9s practice was about to begin, and Stevie had arrived. He wasn't as big and strong as some of their other players but often kids grew a lot at a later age. This boy was quiet but Dave could see the focus in his eyes. He wasn't there to mess around – he was there to show what he could do.

In the sprinting tests, Stevie was one of the quickest and in the passing exercises, he showed that he had good technique. Dave was impressed but he was waiting to see him in the five-a-side match at the end

– that was the real test. It took Stevie a few minutes to get involved but soon he was running the show. He won the ball back and ran forward. He looked up, played a good pass and then moved into space.

Dave looked at Hughie and nodded – he didn't need to say anything.

Stevie was everywhere: rushing back to defend and then rushing forward to shoot. This was only his first session but he was already a leader, showing his teammates where he wanted them to be for the pass. His self-belief and ambition were clear for all to see. These were the very important qualities that the coaches looked for in their young players.

'Wow, that kid's a natural,' Steve said when the practice was over. 'I don't think he played one bad pass.'

'And what a tackler!' Hughie added with a big smile on his face. 'Did anyone ever get past him?'

Dave shook his head. 'He's special, that's for sure. Let's get him back next week.'

*   *   *

'Well played today!' Stevie said to his teammates Michael Owen and Jason Koumas after another win for the Liverpool youth team. Michael was a brilliant striker who scored lots and lots of goals. Stevie had never seen anyone who was so good at finishing. Jason was a skilful midfielder who loved doing tricks and setting up lots of goals. Together, the three of them had a great understanding of each other's abilities on the pitch.

'You too, mate,' Michael replied as they walked to the changing room. 'Do you ever get tired? I get tired just watching you racing around the pitch!'

It was a dream come true for Stevie to be playing for Liverpool, the club he loved. There was a nice, friendly atmosphere there, and Dave, Hughie and Steve were great coaches. With their support and guidance, he was rapidly improving as a central midfielder. When he watched the first team play on the Kop, Stevie thought about the path ahead. The top was a long way off, but he was well on his way.

At Whiston Juniors, Stevie's performances had attracted lots of attention from Premier League scouts. He had a rare combination of skills: passing, shooting, dribbling *and* tackling. Ben wanted to keep his superstar but he also knew that Stevie was destined for bigger things. Manchester United, West Ham and Everton were all interested but when Dave asked him to train with Liverpool, Stevie's mind was made up.

'There's no better place to play than Anfield!' Paul Sr told Stevie. To have a son playing for Liverpool was a thrill for him too. Paul Sr and Julie made sure that Stevie always looked smart and behaved himself, as respect was very important at a club like Liverpool.

From his first training session with the Under-9s, Stevie knew that this was where he wanted to be. He was working hard and competing with other really good young players. Like him, they loved winning and absolutely hated losing. Even when Stevie was exhausted, he never stopped.

'So what shirts are we wearing on Wednesday?' Jason asked.

For the five-a-side matches at the end of training,

the boys were put into teams based on the colour of their shirts. The skills and possession exercises were brilliant too but the half-an-hour match was what everyone looked forward to. Stevie, Michael and Jason made sure that they wore the same kit, so that they were always on the same team. No-one could beat them when they played together. Stevie won the ball and passed to Jason. Jason dribbled past defenders and passed to Michael. Michael always scored.

'Let's wear the grey Liverpool away shirt,' Michael said and they all agreed.

CHAPTER 6

HILLSBOROUGH

Eight-year-old Stevie sat in the living room with his parents and his brother. No-one said a word as they watched the tragic images from the Hillsborough stadium in Sheffield. Liverpool were about to play in the semi-finals of the FA Cup against Nottingham Forest. It was supposed to be an exciting day for the club but something terrible had happened.

Too many fans had been let into the stadium at the last minute and there was an awful crush. Stevie was so shocked by what he saw on the screen. The BBC reported that many people had died. Ninety-six. No-one could believe it.

'How did this happen?' Julie said to no-one in

particular. There were tears in her eyes. 'I hope we don't know anyone that went to the game today.'

Stevie found it very difficult to sleep that night. He couldn't stop thinking about the disaster. The horrible images kept running through his head.

The next morning, there was a knock at the door. People didn't usually come to see them so early on a Sunday. Stevie ran downstairs and opened it. It was Granddad Tony and he looked very upset as he walked into the living room. He didn't say anything until the rest of the family had sat down. As he waited, Stevie was very worried.

'I'm sorry, I've got some really bad news,' Tony began. His voice was shaking with emotion. 'Jon-Paul was one of the ninety-six at Hillsborough.'

Stevie didn't even know that his cousin had gone to the game. He went to Anfield all the time but his mum had bought him a ticket for the semi-final as a special treat. Jon-Paul lived on a different estate in Liverpool but he often came to play at Happy Street with Paul Jr and Stevie. They all loved football and

Liverpool Football Club in particular. They were more like brothers than cousins.

Again, there was silence at 10 Ironside Road, as they tried to take in the terrible news. There was a lot of crying and a great deal of anger and confusion. The Hillsborough disaster was a heartbreaking day for Liverpool: for the city, the football club and the Gerrard family. Stevie would never forget the 15th April, 1989, or his wonderful cousin Jon-Paul.

Jon-Paul was only ten years old, the youngest victim of the tragedy. He wasn't much older than Stevie when he travelled to Sheffield. On a different day, Stevie could have been with him at Hillsborough. He felt so lucky to be alive.

'Are you okay, love?' Julie asked him, squeezing his hand. This was such a difficult thing for a young child to understand. Stevie nodded but he couldn't speak.

When he went back to training a week later, Stevie was more determined than ever to succeed. The football club was still mourning the loss of ninety-six fans but the players had to carry on and show lots of strength. Stevie had an amazing opportunity to do something that would make Jon-Paul and the rest of the family so proud.

He would become a Liverpool hero and he would do it for Jon-Paul.

CHAPTER 7

A VERY LUCKY BOY

Playing for Liverpool never stopped Stevie from playing on Happy Street. If he was at home and he wasn't too tired, he would walk out of his front door and see if there was a game going on. There was almost always someone there with a ball.

'Stevie!' the others cheered whenever he turned up. The local kids were very proud of their friend who showed all the potential of becoming a top Liverpool player, but they never went easy on him. They tackled hard and they took the matches very seriously. This was their Anfield and they wanted to show Stevie that he wasn't the only talented player on the Bluebell Estate.

'Do you think you're too good for us now that you're a star?' they teased him.

'I've always been too good for you!' Stevie teased back.

One day, he was having a kick-about with Mark and the ball rolled into a nettle bush along the side of the pitch.

'I'll get stung if I put my arm in there,' Stevie said. He was wearing a short-sleeved shirt and so he pulled his socks up as high as possible and tried to get the ball with his foot instead.

The nettles were too thick and Stevie couldn't see the ball. He was getting annoyed because he wanted to keep playing. He kicked as hard as he could and his right foot hit something.

Owwwwwwwwwwwwwwwwwwwwwwwwwwwwwww-www!!!

Stevie fell to the ground in agony. He had never felt pain like this. 'Mark, help me! I can't get my leg out of the bush!'

Mark took a look and nearly fell to the ground too. 'Stevie, you've got to stay really still, okay? I'm going to get help.'

Finally, Stevie managed to look down; a big, rusty garden fork was stuck in his big toe. It was even worse than he had expected. A neighbour came down and tried to pull it out but he couldn't. Stevie screamed and cried. This was really bad. What if he could never play football again?

'Don't worry son, we're here!' his dad shouted as he ran over. Stevie could see the worry in Paul Sr's face.

An ambulance arrived and took Stevie to the hospital. It was the worst journey of his life. Every bump in the road was so painful.

'Slow down!' he screamed each time.

The doctor was very worried. 'The toe may well be infected and so we're going to have to take it off,' he told Paul Sr and Julie, but Stevie heard the scary news too.

Paul Sr wasn't happy about that idea and so he called Steve Heighway, the Liverpool youth coach.

'Stevie's had an accident and they're talking about amputating his toe!'

Steve drove straight to the hospital with the Liverpool physio Mark Waller and they tried to change the doctor's mind. 'The kid's football career will be over if you do that. Please try everything else first.'

The surgeon agreed to remove the fork and then look at the damage. There was a big hole there, but Stevie would be able to keep his big toe.

'You're a very lucky boy,' his coach told him when he woke up after the surgery. 'Please don't play on that pitch ever again!'

After five weeks of rest, Stevie was able to play football again. Those were the most boring weeks of his life. The only good things were that he missed lots of school and he watched lots of football on TV.

When he returned to Liverpool Academy, Stevie worked really hard to get back to fitness. Football was the most important thing in the world to him, and after nearly losing his toe, he was more determined than ever.

'Stevie, it's just a practice,' the coaches shouted at him. 'Go easy on your teammates!'

He needed to calm down before he injured himself or someone else.

'You can't tackle like that all the time,' Steve Heighway told him. 'You've got to learn to control yourself and know when to dive in. We know how competitive you are but if you're not careful, you'll get hurt or sent off.'

Stevie listened carefully to his coaches. He was always keen to learn new things, even when everything was going well. The Liverpool Under-12s were winning every week. Stevie and Michael were the perfect partnership in attack – neither of them very tall for their age but with the pace, confidence and talent to beat much bigger teams. Every time Stevie played a great pass, Michael would score.

'It's great to have you back!' Michael said as they celebrated another goal.

Every summer, Liverpool sent out letters to the players that they wanted to come back for the next season. Even though Stevie was one of its rising stars, it was a nervous wait for him.

'There's no need for you to worry,' Steve reassured him at the end of one training session. 'You're going to be our captain.'

Stevie couldn't wait to tell his family the great news. He was the new leader of Liverpool Boys.

'Congratulations son, we're so proud of you!' his dad said when Stevie got home.

'Are you sure they were talking about the right player?' Paul joked with him. He always liked to wind up his younger brother. 'It must be a very bad team!'

Stevie laughed. The future was looking very bright indeed.

CHAPTER 8

LIVERPOOL VS. LILLESHALL

'Come in, lads,' Steve Heighway shouted through the door at the Liverpool training ground.

Stevie was standing outside with Michael Owen and two other teammates, Stephen Wright and Neil Murphy. Sometimes it was bad news if you got called to the coach's office but today the four of them were hoping for some really good news.

'Well done boys,' Steve Heighway said, 'you've been invited to trials at Lilleshall!'

Stevie couldn't believe it. Lilleshall was the National School where the top young English footballers went for the best coaching. Every kid dreamed of going to Lilleshall – there was no better place to develop as a player. Now Stevie, Wrighty and Michael would have the chance to be selected.

'It's going to be so competitive but we can do it,' Michael said with lots of confidence.

'You're right – we play for Liverpool, the best team in England!' Stevie shouted with a huge smile on his face.

There were many highly talented youngsters at the trials but both Stevie and Michael sailed through each round. Hundreds of hopefuls were reduced to fifty, then to twenty-four, but they were both still there. It was really hard work but they believed in themselves.

'I don't think there are any better strikers here but I hope they don't think I'm too small,' Michael said.

'When you're that quick and that good at shooting, it doesn't matter how tall you are!' Stevie replied. 'In midfield, there are some big, strong boys but I'm the best passer and the best tackler.'

'I've never seen anyone so brave!' Michael added.

Stevie was very impatient as he waited for the Lilleshall letter to arrive. Just one final trial awaited him, and he was desperate to get the invitation.

Every day, he ran out of the house to meet the postman, hoping for good news.

'Has the letter arrived?' Stevie asked, out of breath.

'Sorry, lad – not today,' the postman replied.

One day, the Lilleshall letter arrived and Paul Sr opened it. Stevie waited at the top of the stairs with his fingers firmly crossed. There was a pause as his dad read the letter.

'What does it say?' Stevie asked impatiently.

There was a sad look on his dad's face. Stevie knew that it was bad news – Lilleshall had rejected him. He ran back upstairs and slammed his bedroom door. He cried and cried, punching his pillow in anger. He was the captain of Liverpool Boys and the best young midfielder in England. How could they crush his dream like that?

Eventually, Paul Sr came up to comfort his son.

'Dad, I'm finished – I don't want to play football anymore!' Stevie said without looking up.

'I'm sorry, son – they've made a mistake,' Paul Sr said, giving his son a hug. 'You're a very good footballer and you did so well to get this far. I don't know why they turned you down, but now you have to show them why they should have picked you. Don't give up.'

Michael was chosen for Lilleshall, which made it all the harder to bear for Stevie. He was pleased for his friend but it still really hurt. Back at Liverpool, Steve Heighway tried to lift the boy's spirits. 'I know you're very upset but I'm so pleased that you're not going to Lilleshall. You're my superstar and I promise you that I can make you a better player than they can.'

Stevie was determined to prove Lilleshall wrong. His journey to the top might be more difficult at Liverpool but nothing could stop him. Seven months later, The National School came to play a match. Stevie couldn't wait.

'Those Lilleshall boys, they think they're better than you,' Paul Sr told his son the night before, to get him pumped up for the big game. But Stevie didn't need any more encouragement; he was ready for the biggest match of his life.

From the first whistle, Stevie flew into tackle after

tackle. The Lilleshall midfield faced a considerable challenge. The referee asked Stevie to calm down but he wasn't listening. Lilleshall won 4–3, with Michael scoring a hat-trick, but Stevie – for Liverpool – had played the best match of his career so far.

'Well played,' the Lilleshall players said as they shook Stevie's hand at the end. They knew how good Stevie was and they were scared of him.

'It's a joke that they didn't select you,' Michael told him as they chatted after the game. 'You're so much better than the others!'

At Liverpool, Steve Heighway looked after Stevie like a son. With the right support, he was sure that his young captain would be a great player for his club and country. Steve took both Stevie and Michael on the Under-18 tour to Spain when they were still playing for the Under-14s.

'It's important for you to get these experiences as early as possible,' Steve told them. 'You're travelling with the team, representing Liverpool against top teams in Europe. You can learn a lot from just watching these games.'

Steve also secured Stevie tickets for Liverpool first team matches. Sometimes, Stevie went to Anfield with his brother but when The Reds made it to a big final, Stevie would travel to Wembley with Steve and his family.

'Liverpool are going to destroy Bolton today!' Stevie said on the train down to London. It was the 1995 Coca-Cola Cup Final and Liverpool, with great players like Jamie Redknapp, John Barnes, Steve McManaman, Ian Rush and Robbie Fowler, were the favourites to win.

As a fifteen-year-old from Huyton, Stevie loved being part of the big crowds heading to Wembley. The fans were all dressed up in their team's colours and everyone was singing songs. Looking up at the massive national stadium in front of him, he dreamed of one day playing there in front of 75,000 fans.

'You'll be out there soon,' Steve Heighway said as they took their seats, reading his mind. 'For Liverpool and for England!'

Liverpool played really well and they had lots of chances to score. With a few minutes left in the first half, McManaman dribbled through the middle. With three defenders in front of him, he used his pace to run around the outside. McManaman cut inside past the last defender and shot into the net.

'What a goal!' Stevie shouted as he celebrated with the other Liverpool fans.

In the second half, McManaman got the ball on the left and ran forward. He cut into the penalty area on his right foot, dribbled past a defender and curled the ball into the bottom corner.

'He's incredible!' Stevie screamed.

McManaman was eight years older than him but Stevie began to picture a future Liverpool team – Jamie Carragher in defence, Gerrard and Redknapp in the centre of midfield, with McManaman on the wing and Fowler and Owen up front. What a team that would be.

CHAPTER 9

PLAYING WITH THE BIG BOYS

The young Liverpool players had to do some work experience. Some of the boys worked at supermarkets or building sites, but Stevie had an alternative idea.

'The older boys told me that sometimes you can do the two weeks at Liverpool,' Stevie said to Steve Heighway. 'I want to do that! I'll do anything – clean boots, mop the floors.'

Steve agreed to sort this out for his star player. When Stevie arrived at Melwood, the Liverpool training ground, he was expecting to do boring tasks in the dressing room. But he was in for a surprise.

'Right, lad, you'll be helping with the first team training today,' one of the coaches told him.

Stevie couldn't believe it. Work experience kids had trained with the reserves in the past but this was even better. He stood on the touchline watching his hero John Barnes up close and it was the best thing he had ever seen. Barnes's skills were just amazing.

'We need another player for the five-a-side match,' the Liverpool manager, Roy Evans, told him, throwing him a yellow bib.

Stevie was speechless. He was sixteen years old and now he was passing the ball to Barnes. Was he dreaming? At the end of the game, Barnes gave him a pat on the back.

'Well played, kid,' he said and Stevie would never forget that moment. He couldn't wait to play with the big boys every day.

Lots of other clubs were taking an interest in Stevie, and he visited a few of them – Everton, Manchester United – to have a look around and play a few practice matches. At Manchester United, he met Alex Ferguson and they tried to sign him, but

Stevie just wanted Liverpool to offer him a contract. There was only one place that he wanted to play football.

'How was Old Trafford?' Steve Heighway asked when Stevie returned. There was no chance that he would let his star player sign for Manchester United.

'It was great,' the youth replied with smile. 'I'm thinking about their offer...'

'You were born to play here at Anfield,' Steve told him.

'I know but I don't have a contract yet...' Stevie said cheekily.

'Leave it with me – I'll get that sorted.'

A few weeks later, Stevie had a Youth Trainee Scheme contract. He would be paid £50 each week to become a professional footballer. He was so proud to sign for the club that he had supported all his life – and his family were delighted too.

'Our son, the Liverpool player!' Paul Sr said at dinner, lifting his glass to raise a toast.

'At this rate, you'll be the smallest player ever to play at Anfield,' Paul Jr joked.

Once he had finished his exams, Stevie started his apprenticeship at Liverpool. Every time he put on the red club shirt, he felt on top of the world. It was the happiest time of his life. Together with friends like Michael, he worked hard and played hard.

As one of the players walked into the dressing room, Michael nodded and Stevie quickly turned the lights off. In the darkness, they flicked their towels at their teammate over and over again.

Owwwwwwww! Stop it!

Hahahahahahahahahaha!

Off the pitch, they were always making fun of each other's clothes but on the pitch, they were a great team. Stevie loved the competitive atmosphere. Everyone always gave 110 per cent.

Training sessions took place at Melwood, right next to the Liverpool first team. Redknapp, McManaman, Fowler and David James were the big stars and they always looked cool. Stevie tried to speak to them whenever he could. He wasn't nervous around them; he wanted to be part of their gang. All of the young players tried to copy everything 'The Spice Boys' did.

One day after training, Jamie Redknapp came over to Stevie. Normally, the senior players only spoke to the young players if they wanted them to get something for them.

'You're a very good player,' Jamie said. 'You're passing is really good and that shot is powerful. Keep it up!'

Stevie was so happy to hear an England international praising him. After that, Jamie often offered him advice about how to be a better midfielder. Stevie listened carefully to every single word.

'Have these,' Jamie said to him one day in the dressing room, and threw him a brand new pair of Mizuno boots. Stevie cleaned Jamie's boots every week and they were the nicest that he had ever seen. He couldn't wait to wear them.

'Thanks, Jamie!' Stevie said with a big smile on his face.

The only problem in those days was the risk of

injuries. Stevie had grown suddenly from a little kid to six feet tall, and his body was struggling to cope with the changes. Sometimes his ankles were sore but he felt most pain in his back and knees. Every time he was playing well, the injuries would return.

'How are you feeling?' the Liverpool physio asked him, touching the different parts of his knees.

Stevie winced with the pain. 'It's not getting any better – this is so frustrating!'

One day when things were really bad, the manager Roy Evans spoke to him. 'I know this is a tough time for you but you have to keep your head up and keep working hard. Everyone here at Liverpool thinks very highly of you. As soon as you get these injuries sorted, you'll be up in the first team, I'm sure.'

Stevie was really pleased to hear that from the Liverpool manager. Sometimes he was unlucky with injuries but sometimes, he just needed to be more sensible, especially in training. He loved to tackle but there was no point in hurting himself just to impress.

'How many times have we told you to calm down?' said Ronnie Moran, one of the Liverpool coaches. 'You're flying into big tackles when you've just come back from injury!'

With the club starting to offer professional contracts to his teammates, Stevie was getting very worried. Liverpool wanted to see him in fit and healthy form, but what if the injuries never went away?

'Dad, this uncertainty is awful!' he complained.

So Paul Sr went to see Steve Heighway. 'As you know, Stevie is really struggling at the moment. All of this contract talk is really affecting his performances. You know how much he wants this – can't we just get it sorted now?'

Steve spoke to Roy Evans, and soon Stevie Gerrard had his first professional contract. It was the best day of his life as he signed the papers. It was the start of great times at Liverpool.

CHAPTER 10

ANOTHER STEP CLOSER

With his contract signed, Stevie got back to doing what he did best – passing the ball, tackling players and scoring goals from midfield. With Jamie's advice in his head, he ran from box to box and never stopped. He was doing well for the Liverpool Under-19s and everyone was talking about him.

'They say that Tottenham want to buy you for £2 million!' said Stephen Wright, or 'Wrighty' as most of the squad called him, at training one day.

It was just a rumour but that was a lot of money for a youngster who had never before played for the first team. Stevie didn't even think about leaving

Liverpool but it was nice to hear that he was
attracting attention.

One morning as he arrived for training, Steve
Heighway asked him to come into his office.

'Stevie, you'll have people watching you this
morning,' he warned. 'Sammy Lee and Patrice
Bergues are coming down to see you in action. Don't
panic – just play your natural game.'

Two of the top Liverpool coaches were coming to
watch him – this was the biggest day of his life. The
new manager, Gérard Houllier had just arrived from
France and he wanted to bring more young players
into the first team squad. This was like a trial and
Stevie was ready to shine.

He worked harder than ever, winning every ball
and playing perfect passes. Most of all, Stevie tried to
take up good positions to receive the ball, and to look
calm in possession. Those were the qualities that he
needed to display to make the next step up. He could
see Sammy and Patrice on the touchline, chatting and
taking notes. Sweat was pouring down Stevie's face
but he kept going right until the end of the session.

As Stevie walked off the pitch, Steve introduced him to Patrice and Sammy.

'Well done, you looked good today,' Sammy said, shaking his hand, and Patrice nodded in agreement.

Stevie couldn't help smiling. He was impressing the right people at the club. Hopefully, Houllier himself would come to watch him soon.

One day, as Stevie warmed up against Manchester United, he saw Houllier standing with the other Liverpool coaches. He took a deep breath – this needed to be his best match yet. With his tough tackling, Stevie won the battle against the United midfield and he showed that he could create lots of chances with his passing too. He capped off a great performance with a powerful strike from the edge of the penalty area. As he celebrated the goal, Stevie looked to the bench but Houllier was gone. He just hoped that the manager had seen enough.

'Did you know Houllier was there today?' Paul Sr asked as he drove Stevie home from the game.

'Of course!' he said with a smile.

'Well, you did very well today, kid,' his dad replied.

A few days later, Steve Heighway called Stevie and Wrighty into his office. 'I've got big news for you, lads. Houllier wants you to train with the first team at Melwood from now on. You start on Monday.'

Stevie and Wrighty looked at each other and smiled. This was it.

'This is a big chance for you,' Steve continued, 'but I want you to always remember your days here in the Academy. You'll need to keep your feet on the ground over the next few months. You're not a Liverpool first team footballer yet.'

Stevie nodded. He was very grateful for all of Steve's guidance over the years and he would always listen to his first coach's advice. Moving to Melwood was only the start – there was plenty of work still to be done.

'Congratulations mate, welcome to the first team!' Jamie said as Stevie arrived in the dressing room. He was nervous and he didn't want to sit in someone else's seat. He looked around for his name but it wasn't written anywhere.

'Over there!' one of the coaches pointed and Stevie sat down in the far corner next to the big bag of footballs. He wasn't one of the big boys yet.

It was the hardest training session that Stevie had endured, but he enjoyed every second of it. He loved to challenge himself and players like McManaman and Fowler were the best around. When practice finished, Houllier asked Stevie and Wrighty to stay behind.

'You're both good players but you need to get bigger and stronger,' the manager told them. 'Right now, you look tiny next to the other players but we'll help you to get to their level. Just listen carefully and don't complain.'

For the first time in his life, Stevie began to think about his diet. He didn't eat lots of fast food but he stopped eating burgers altogether. Instead, he ate more pasta and salads. Stevie needed to get really serious about football, and – as they kept telling him, 'live like an athlete'.

'This is so boring!' Wrighty said, as he rested after lifting weights in the club gym. Every day, the pair did football training in the morning and then strength training in the afternoon. It was really hard work but Stevie was focused on achieving his goals.

'Next time you lift that bar, picture standing in the tunnel for your Liverpool debut,' Stevie told Wrighty. 'That's what I do. I imagine myself touching the "This is Anfield" sign with the noise of fans all around me. It will be the best day of our lives and every weights session gets us closer to that day.'

In November 1998, Liverpool were playing in the UEFA Cup and for their third round match against Celta Vigo, Houllier invited Stevie and Wrighty to travel with the squad.

'We're going to Spain!' Wrighty cheered loudly.

They didn't expect to play in the game but it would be a great experience to be around the first team players. Stevie shared a hotel room with Jamie Redknapp and continued to learn from him. He watched what he did, what he said and what he ate. There was so much to learn.

On the day of the match, Stevie walked into the dressing room and there was a shirt with his name on it – '28 GERRARD'. He couldn't believe it. He was going to be a Liverpool substitute. Only a month earlier, he had been playing for the Under-19s.

Liverpool lost 3–1 and Stevie didn't actually get to play, but he learnt a lot from the game. Claude Makélélé was the defensive midfielder for Celta Vigo and he calmly controlled the match, passing forward to his more skilful teammates. He made it look so easy. It was the kind of neat, possession football that Stevie wanted to excel at. Now, he was getting so close to that Liverpool debut.

CHAPTER 11

THE DEBUT

'Incey, you better watch out – Stevie's going to take your place!' Jamie joked in training.

Paul Ince was Jamie's partner in central midfield and he was an England international. But Stevie was fearless and he was doing everything he could to win his Liverpool debut.

For Liverpool's Premier League match against Blackburn in November 1998, Stevie was included in the eighteen-man squad for the very first time. It was great news but he didn't get excited until he made the final sixteen.

'Houllier thinks you can play central midfield, right-back or right midfield,' Jamie said to him. 'That makes you a great substitute to have. Be ready to come on!'

Liverpool were winning 2–0 and Houllier sent the subs out to warm up along the touchline. The atmosphere was brilliant at Anfield and the fans clapped them as they ran along and did some stretches. Did they know who Stevie was? He doubted it; to them, he was probably a skinny kid who would never make it to the top.

'I'll show them,' he said to himself.

With a few minutes to go, Stevie thought he would have to wait another week for his debut. But then Sammy Lee called his name.

'You're coming on, lad!'

As he stood on the touchline, Stevie tucked his shirt in and tried to stay calm. His heart was beating so fast. This was the moment that he had been dreaming about for years.

'Good luck, kid!' teammate Phil Thompson said. 'You'll be playing at right-back.'

'Keep the ball, there's not long to go,' Houllier told him.

When the ball came to Stevie, he controlled it carefully and played a simple pass to another teammate. The relief was incredible. He hadn't made a mistake with his first touches. A few seconds later, Incey played a ball to him down the wing. Stevie had a great chance to cross the ball into the box. It was something he had done so many times before but this was different. With the pressure on, he put far too much power on the cross and it sailed out for a goal kick. The Liverpool fans groaned.

'Sorry!' he shouted to his teammates.

When the referee blew the final whistle, Stevie relaxed. Now, he could finally enjoy his big day.

'Well done, mate. How was that?' Michael said, as they hugged on the pitch.

'I've never been so nervous,' Stevie admitted. 'Incey won't let me forget that awful cross for years!'

Michael had made his first team debut at seventeen, and now Stevie had done it at eighteen. They were the future of Liverpool Football Club and it was so exciting.

All of his teammates congratulated Stevie in the dressing room, especially Jamie. Now, he really felt like part of the team. As soon as he was changed, he went out into the players' lounge to see his family.

'Well done, son!' Paul Sr shouted as soon as he saw him.

'What was that cross about?' Paul Jr joked.

Even his brother's teasing couldn't take the smile off Stevie's face. He was officially a Liverpool first team footballer now and that was the best feeling in the world.

A week later, Stevie started in the match against Tottenham. He had hoped to play in his favourite central midfield role this time but when he saw the team sheet, he saw that he was at right-back again. And against Spurs, that meant a very difficult opponent – David Ginola. Ginola was a really skilful winger and he was much stronger than Stevie too. He tried really hard to tackle him but the Frenchman was just too good. Stevie was having a nightmare match and he wanted it to be over.

'Keep going!' Jamie shouted to him.

By the end of the match, Stevie thought his
Liverpool career was over. Surely Houllier would
decide that he wasn't good enough for the first team.
But instead, the manager came up to him and patted
him on the back.

'That was a very tough game but you did okay,'
Houllier said to him. 'You didn't give up and you
showed the character that we're looking for.'

It felt great to have so much support from the
players and coaches. There was a real family
atmosphere at Liverpool and Stevie loved it.
Everyone believed in him and, with every minute he
was on the pitch, he was learning so much.

When Jamie got injured, Stevie finally got the
chance to play in central midfield. He felt much
more comfortable in his normal position, running
up and down through the centre of the pitch.
He had so much energy and he wasn't afraid of
anything. Against Middlesbrough, he was up against
one of his childhood heroes, Paul Gascoigne. He
could remember watching him at Euro 96 on TV
back on the Bluebell Estate. In the first minute of

this match, though, Gazza ran into him and hit him right in the face.

'Owwwwwwwwww!' Stevie screamed. His face was throbbing with pain. He would have a great black eye in the morning.

He was only a youngster and Gazza was an England legend but Stevie flew into the next tackle. Gazza skipped past him but the game became a battle between the two of them. Liverpool won and at the end of the match, Gazza approached him.

'You're a really good player,' he said, putting an arm around Stevie. 'Keep playing like that and you'll be a star.'

That was the best thing Stevie had ever heard. He couldn't wait to tell his family; his brother would be so jealous.

By the end of the 1998–99 season, Stevie had played in twelve Premier League matches and a few European games too. He was having the time of his life and the fans were chanting his name.

'Next year, my aim is to become Houllier's first choice in central midfield,' he told Michael.

'What about Incey and Jamie?' his friend asked.

'What about them?!' Stevie replied. He was full of confidence.

CHAPTER 12

BOX TO BOX

'What did I tell you?' Stevie said to Michael with a smile. Incey had been sold to Middlesbrough in the summer of 1999 and Stevie was now Jamie's regular partner in midfield. While Jamie played the nice passes and set up goals, Stevie ran everywhere and did lots of tackling.

'Yes, you were right about that,' Michael said, 'but are you ever going to score any goals? You used to take lots of shots for the youth team but now you hardly ever cross the halfway line.'

His friend was right; Stevie needed to show the Liverpool coaches that he could really attack as well as defend. With his pace, he could burst forward from midfield and help out the strikers. But if he ever got into good positions, he panicked and passed the ball, or shot high over the bar.

'All I need is that first goal,' Stevie explained to Michael. 'Once I have that, I think I'll feel much more confident.'

At home to Sheffield Wednesday in December 1999, Liverpool were 2–0 up with twenty minutes to go. With Jamie injured, Didi Hamann was playing in defensive midfield and Stevie was told to push forward. This was his chance to show what he could do.

Stevie ran quickly towards the heart of the Sheffield Wednesday defence. They weren't ready for his pace and he glided past one man and then another. He was in the penalty area with only the goalkeeper to beat. This was when he needed to stay calm. He imagined that he was still back at Happy Street, pretending to be John Barnes with his mates. His shot was low and hard, and right into the bottom corner of the net.

Goooooooooooooooooaaaaaaaaaaaaaaaaaaaaaaaaaa aalllllllllllllllllllllllllllllllllll!!!!

Stevie had done it! He slid along the grass towards the fans and his teammates jumped on top of him. He could hear the fans chanting his name. Nothing could beat that feeling.

'What a run!' Didi shouted. 'I didn't know you could dribble like that.'

Suddenly, Stevie wasn't just a tough tackler; he was an attacker too. If they beat Arsenal, Liverpool could climb to third in the table. Again, Didi played slightly deeper and Houllier asked Stevie to be more creative.

After fifteen minutes of the Arsenal game, Stevie secured the ball in his own half. As he looked up, he saw Titi Camara making a brilliant run behind the Arsenal defence. Stevie would need to deliver an amazing pass, but he had been famous for his long passes in the Liverpool youth team. This was the perfect time to see if he could do it at the highest level.

So he curled the ball past the Arsenal defenders and straight into Titi's path. The striker ran towards goal and shot past the keeper, David Seaman. Liverpool were winning.

In the second half, the Arsenal midfielder Freddie Ljungberg ran through on goal. He took the ball around the goalkeeper and he looked certain to score the equaliser. But just as he was about to shoot, Stevie ran in and made a brilliant tackle. When the final whistle went, Stevie was the match-winner.

'That's one of the best performances I've ever seen,' Didi said as they celebrated with the fans.

Stevie was really pleased with the way that he was developing as a player. He was an all-round midfielder now who could tackle, pass, *and* shoot. He was a regular for the England Under-21 team but there were rumours that the senior England manager, Kevin Keegan, was watching him too.

'You'd be great with Paul Scholes in midfield,' Michael Owen said excitedly. After his brilliant goals at World Cup 1998, Michael was a regular for the England team and he wanted his friend Stevie playing with him.

One day, Paul Jr called Stevie and told him to phone Steve Heighway.

'What's going on?' asked Stevie.

'Congratulations, kid,' Steve told him happily. 'Keegan wants you to go and train with the England squad before the friendly against Argentina.'

Stevie was so excited. He understood that he wouldn't play in the match but it was a big step forward just to be around the team. If he did well in the practices, perhaps he would be called up to the next squad.

As he drove to the training camp, Stevie got more and more nervous. He was only nineteen years old and he would be joining really experienced, world-class players like Sol Campbell, David Beckham and Alan Shearer. Was he good enough, though? When he arrived at the hotel, Stevie called Jamie who was already downstairs at dinner.

'Mate, can you help me please?' he said. 'I'm really worried about making a fool of myself.'

Jamie ran upstairs. 'Come on, there's nothing to worry about. Keegan called you up because he thinks you're good enough,' he said, pushing Stevie towards the stairs. 'I think you're good enough, Michael thinks you're good enough, Robbie thinks you're good enough – so you're good enough!'

Keegan introduced Stevie to all of the players. The youth could barely stand up because he was shaking so much, but he soon felt more at ease as everyone was really friendly. On the training field, he loved how competitive everyone was. There were lots of tough tackles and arguments.

The talent was a joy to watch. Shearer could score in the top corner every time; Beckham could cross the ball perfectly on to the striker's head; and Scholes could always see space before everyone else and play a really clever pass. Stevie had a long way to go to reach their level but he would do everything he could to get there.

One day, in May 2000, as he walked through Liverpool with his dad, Stevie's phone rang.

'Hello?'

'Hi Stevie, this is Kevin Keegan,' the voice on the other end said.

At first, he thought it was a teammate playing a joke but soon, Stevie realised that it really was Keegan calling.

'I'm calling you up for the game on Wednesday,' the England Manager told him, and Stevie felt like dancing through the city streets. 'See you at the team hotel.'

England's opponents would be Ukraine. At the training camp, Stevie worked hard and just hoped that he would get to play. Keegan came over to talk to him on the day before the game.

'Are you excited about tomorrow night?' he asked.

'Of course, I can't wait!' Stevie replied.

'Good, because you're starting,' Keegan said.

Stevie couldn't believe it. He'd be playing in midfield with Beckham, Scholes and McManaman. That was a terrifying thought. The next twenty-four hours went by very slowly. Stevie just wanted to get out onto the pitch and make his England debut.

In the dressing room, Stevie had never heard so much passion and shouting before a match. It was the best atmosphere ever and it only got better as they came out of the tunnel.

For eighty minutes, Stevie ran and ran across the beautiful Wembley grass. Ukraine had great players like Andriy Shevchenko but he didn't let them have time on the ball. Stevie made some good tackles and he ran forward to support the strikers when he could. It wasn't a spectacular debut but it was a solid one. As he left the pitch, the England fans clapped and cheered.

'Well played, lad,' Keegan said as he went to sit down on the bench.

Stevie just hoped that he had done enough to make the England squad for Euro 2000.

CHAPTER 13

AN AMAZING YEAR

'I'm in – I'm coming to Belgium and Holland with you!' Stevie told Michael. Having just turned twenty years old, this was beyond Stevie's wildest dreams. He couldn't wait for their big Euro 2000 adventure to begin.

As he arrived at the England camp, Stevie was full of high hopes for the tournament but a few days later, he really missed home. He had never been away for so long before.

'Why don't you speak to your parents?' Michael suggested. 'I find it always helps to hear a friendly voice and talk about family things. You'll be back in Liverpool in no time.'

His teammates were really kind and invited him to play snooker and card games with them. Once he was working really hard to impress the coaches, he had no time to feel homesick. Portugal had world-class attackers like Rui Costa and Luís Figo, and he knew that Incey and Scholesy had lots more experience of playing in big matches. Stevie watched from the bench as England lost 3–2.

It meant that they would need a victory in their next game. Early in the second half against Germany, Alan Shearer headed the ball into the net. 1–0! Ten minutes later, Keegan made a substitution to protect the lead.

'Stevie, go and get warmed up!' one of the coaches shouted and his heart started beating a lot faster.

His job was to come on and make lots of tackles to try and stop the Germans from scoring. There was a lot of pressure on Stevie but tackling was what he was born to do. He warmed up every muscle in his body – he was ready for the challenge.

As he ran on, Stevie listened to the incredible noise of the England fans. He was nervous but he was also looking forward to the battle. He raced around the pitch, blocking passes and stopping attacks. He vowed that no-one was getting past him. By the final whistle, the atmosphere was incredible. England had beaten Germany.

'Congratulations, mate,' Didi Hamann, Stevie's teammate at Liverpool, said as they swapped shirts. 'You played really well.'

'What a performance, lad!' Keegan said, giving Stevie a big hug.

It felt so good to be part of the victory. The next day, the national newspapers called Stevie 'England's future' and 'an England captain in the making'. It was a very proud moment.

Keegan wanted his new star to play in the last group match against Romania but Stevie had hurt his calf in the Germany match. Without him, England lost 3–2 and crashed out of the tournament. It was a very disappointing end but Stevie was excited about the next Premier League season.

It was great to be back in Liverpool. Houllier was building a strong team, with Sami Hyypiä and Jamie

Carragher in defence, Didi and Stevie in midfield and Michael, Emile Heskey and Robbie Fowler up front. When Scottish midfielder Gary McAllister signed from Coventry, everyone was surprised.

'Why have we bought him? He's old!' Stevie said at training when they heard the news.

But Macca was very experienced and Stevie learnt a lot from listening to him, especially about calmly picking the best pass. Stevie sometimes had so much energy that he moved too fast without thinking.

'Be smarter with the ball,' Macca advised him again and again. 'Keep possession – if you can't play a good long pass, play a safe short pass instead.'

With great players and coaches around him, Stevie was getting better and better. After Euro 2000, he was determined to live up to the hype. Sometimes he still got too angry in big matches but he was scoring more goals and Liverpool were playing well in all competitions. In February 2001, they won the League Cup and in May, they made it to two more finals.

First came the FA Cup Final against Arsenal. The Gunners took the lead after seventy minutes.

'Come on, we've got to keep going,' Stevie told his teammates as they stood around with their heads down. He was still young but he was showing clear signs of leadership. 'It's not over yet!'

Macca crossed a free-kick into the box and Michael smashed the ball into the net. The game was heading for extra time but Patrik Berger played a beautiful long pass for Michael to run on to. He was far too quick for the Arsenal defenders and he calmly slotted the ball past the goalkeeper. At the final whistle, the Liverpool players hugged each other. It was an amazing team victory over a brilliant Arsenal side.

'Right, we've won the double,' Stevie said to Michael once he had kissed the cup. 'Now for the treble!'

Having reached the UEFA Cup Final, Liverpool were favourites to beat the Spanish side Alavés. After fifteen minutes, Michael got the ball in attack and Stevie made a brilliant run from midfield. When the pass arrived, he took one touch and calmly struck the ball into the bottom corner.

Gooooooooooooooooaaaaaaaaaaaaaaaaaaaaallllllllllll llllllllllllllllllllllllllllll!!!!!!!!!!!!

Stevie and Michael celebrated another great Liverpool team goal with the fans. At half-time, Liverpool were leading 3–1 but in the second half, the Spanish team began to catch up. The score was 4–4 after ninety minutes. It had been a very exciting game and the players were exhausted.

'We don't want this to go to penalties,' Stevie told his teammates as they sat on the grass and stretched their legs. 'Let's get a winner in extra time.'

With three minutes to go, Alavés scored an own goal. It was a cruel way to lose but Liverpool had their third trophy of the season. As Robbie and Sami lifted the trophy, red confetti flew up into the night air and Stevie jumped up and down with his teammates.

What an amazing season it had been. Stevie had three winners' medals and he was named the PFA Young Player of the Year too. Could it get any better?

'Next up, The Premier League title and the Champions League!' he told Michael.

CHAPTER 14

CAPTAIN OF LIVERPOOL

Stevie signed a big new contract at Liverpool. 'This is my home!' he told the fans happily.

Everything was going so well for him but one problem remained – he had to stop getting sent off for dangerous tackles.

'That was really stupid,' Macca told him after another red card against Aston Villa. Stevie had let his team down and he felt very ashamed. 'When you get frustrated, you can't just do that. You have to think about when to tackle hard and when to take a deep breath and walk away.'

'You're my vice-captain now,' Houllier told Stevie, 'and so you have to lead by example.' The player could hear the disappointment in his manager's voice. 'You'll be a great Liverpool captain soon,' Houllier went on, 'but only if you calm down on the pitch.'

Stevie listened to all of the advice and began to learn from his mistakes. He was still young but there were no excuses for his behaviour. Aggression and bravery were very important parts of his playing style but if he didn't learn to control his temper, he could hurt other players and he could hurt himself too. As a result of a groin injury, he had to miss the 2002 World Cup in South Korea and Japan.

'I can't keep playing like this,' Stevie said to himself.

He was really upset to be watching the tournament on TV. He had played a key role in England's great qualifying campaign, notably at the Olympiastadion in Munich. Germany had taken the lead after six minutes but Michael scored an equaliser. In the last minute of the first half, a Beckham cross was headed out to Stevie, who was at least thirty yards from goal.

Stevie had nothing to lose. He chested the ball down and struck a powerful shot. The ball flew through the air, bounced and then zipped along into the bottom corner. The goalkeeper had no chance.

Goooooooooooooooooooooooaaaaaaaaaaaaaaaaaa aaaaaallllllllllllllllllllllllllllll!!!!!

It was Stevie's first goal for England – and what a goal it was. He ran towards the corner flag and then dived along the grass. His teammates were right behind him and jumped on top of him.

'What a shot!'

'That's a worldie!'

The game finished 5–1 to England, with Michael scoring a hat-trick. It was one of the best days of Stevie's life.

Now, Stevie focused on getting fit for the new Premier League season. He needed to show that he was more mature now.

Liverpool weren't playing well in the Premiership but they were through to the League Cup Final again. This time, they were up against massive rivals Manchester United. Stevie couldn't wait.

'There's nothing like beating United!' he told Michael in the dressing room before kick-off. 'When I was a young Liverpool fan, they were always the games I wanted to win most. Now, I get to play and win the games myself!'

As the first half came to an end, Stevie got the ball about thirty yards out. That first England goal had shown the fans that he was brilliant at shooting from long range. They wanted to see another great strike.

Shoot! Shoot!

Beckham ran out to close him down but Stevie's shot deflected off his leg and rocketed into the top corner. In his excitement, Stevie took his shirt off and ran towards the fans. In the biggest match of their season, he had scored the first goal.

Stevie ran and ran to stop the Manchester United attacks. Jerzy Dudek made some great saves but Liverpool still needed a second goal. On the counter-attack, Didi played a great pass to Michael and he shot past Fabien Barthez.

'That's it – we've won!' Stevie shouted, giving Michael a big hug.

It felt so good to beat Manchester United, especially in a cup final. It was another winner's medal for Stevie but it wasn't the one that he really wanted.

'We're great in cup competitions but why can't we do well over thirty-eight matches in the Premier League?' he asked Michael.

'We need to be more consistent,' Michael replied. 'We have to win the less important games too.'

They both loved Liverpool Football Club but the team needed to change their way of thinking in order to reach the next level. It was all about belief and the desire to win. Stevie and Michael had these qualities but did all of the others?

Houllier was thinking about changes too.

'Come and see me after training,' he said to Stevie as they got ready for the season ahead.

In his office, Houllier was sitting with his assistant, Phil Thompson. 'Stevie, we've been talking to the coaches and a few of the players and we've decided to try a new captain,' Houllier explained. 'We think you're ready to take on the responsibility.'

Stevie couldn't believe it – it was a massive honour for a twenty-three-year-old, especially one who was a local lad and a big Liverpool fan. He had always dreamt of being the club captain, leading his team out onto the pitch at Anfield.

'Thanks, I won't let the club down!' he told Houllier with a big smile on his face.

CHAPTER 15

THINKING ABOUT THE FUTURE

'We've got a great chance at this tournament,' Stevie said to Michael as they made their way to Portugal for Euro 2004. 'This is our best squad for years!'

David Beckham, Scholesy and Sol Campbell were experienced, older players and there were lots of very good younger players too like Frank Lampard, John Terry, Wayne Rooney, Stevie and Michael. Everyone got on really well and there were lots of practical jokes and card games to amuse them while they waited for the tournament to begin.

England's first match was against a France team featuring Zinedine Zidane, Thierry Henry and Patrick

Vieira. They would have to be on top form to beat the French.

'They're good but we've got nothing to fear,' Beckham told his teammates in the dressing room before kick-off. 'We're as good as anyone – let's make our country proud!'

The players roared like lions and prepared for battle. The atmosphere in the stadium was amazing. Stevie looked up and there seemed to be England fans everywhere, waving their white flags with the red cross of St George. Frank scored a header in the first half and even when Beckham missed a penalty, it looked like England would get a great first win.

In the last few minutes of the match, though, France won a free-kick. Zidane stepped up and hit a perfect shot into the corner of the net. The England players were disappointed but a draw would be a good result.

'Keep your heads up, boys,' Becks shouted. 'We just need to hold on for a few more minutes.'

The ball came to Stevie and he tried to play it back to the goalkeeper, David James. But he hadn't seen Henry's clever run to intercept the pass. Stevie watched in horror as Henry beat James to the ball and the goalkeeper brought him down. Penalty! Zidane scored to win the match for France.

'Don't worry,' Michael said to Stevie. In the dressing room, he was silent, thinking about how he had let the team down with that awful error. 'Forget about it and move on to the next match.'

Against Switzerland, Wayne scored two great goals and then Stevie got a third. It was a relief to help his country towards victory this time.

'I think they've forgiven you!' Michael joked as the England supporters cheered Stevie's goal loudly.

England made it through to the quarter-finals against Portugal. As hosts of the tournament, Portugal had a massive swell of home support, and their team's wingers, Luis Figo and Cristiano Ronaldo, were very skilful.

'We can do this!' Becks shouted in the dressing room and the players echoed his belief. This was their chance to shine. After thirty-eight years, it was time for England to win another trophy.

They had the perfect start when Michael scored in the third minute but then Wayne Rooney got injured. With England's star player off the pitch, the opposition grew more and more confident.

'Keep going, lads!' Stevie shouted as he chased after Portugal's skilful midfielders with sweat pouring down his face. He worked so hard in the summer heat that with ten minutes to go, Stevie had to come off. Only a minute later, Portugal equalised.

As he sat on the bench, Stevie held his head in his hands. He was so nervous that he could barely watch the match. In extra time, Portugal took the lead but Frank Lampard scored to take the match to penalties.

'Come on, you can do this!' Stevie said, patting everyone on the back. Normally, he would have been one of the takers and he wished that he could take one now.

After twelve penalties, it was 5–5. The tension was incredible. The whole team stood together on the halfway line to watch. They were into sudden death and when Darius Vassell's shot was saved, the Portuguese goalkeeper scored to win the match.

It was so disappointing to lose, especially on penalties. There were tears in everyone's eyes and no-one knew what to say. It was a very sad, quiet dressing room after the game but Wayne raised everyone's spirits.

'Don't worry, boys – that was just the warm-up for the 2006 World Cup!'

As Stevie returned to Liverpool, he thought long and hard about his future. He loved his local club but he was very ambitious. He wanted to be challenging for the Premiership and the Champions League. There were three big English clubs – Arsenal, Manchester United and Chelsea – and Liverpool lay a long way behind them.

'We finished thirty points behind Arsenal last season,' he said to his dad. 'That's just not good enough.'

'I know, son, but why don't you give Rafa one season to change your mind?' Paul Sr suggested.

Rafa Benitez had become the new manager of Liverpool in 2004 and the players were very excited to have such a big name in charge.

'He's a top coach,' Jamie Carragher said. 'His teams are strong, fit and very skilful. Every time we've played Valencia, they've destroyed us!'

Rafa had won the Spanish league twice in three years with Valencia, as well as the UEFA Cup. He was a winner and that's what Stevie and Liverpool needed.

Rafa visited Stevie, Michael and Carra at the England camp in Portugal. He said: 'I firmly believe that I can bring success to Liverpool but I need my best players to believe in me and work hard for me.'

Stevie was impressed by Rafa's plans for the club but meanwhile Chelsea were trying really hard to sign him. In Portugal, Frank Lampard and John Terry kept telling him about life at Stamford Bridge.

'It's the best! With Abramovich as chairman and Mourinho as manager, there's lots of money for new signings and we're going to win every trophy around,' Frank told Stevie confidently.

It was a very tempting offer but Stevie's family were desperate for him to stay at Liverpool.

'You've got to stay,' Paul Jr told his brother. 'You'll

hate it in London and Rafa's about to turn Liverpool into a quality side.'

In the end, Stevie decided to stay but he wanted to see improvements at Liverpool.

'You've made the right decision,' Rafa told him, patting him on the back. 'Together, we'll bring lots more trophies to Anfield.'

CHAPTER 16

CHAMPIONS OF EUROPE

'These new signings are really good!' Carra said after a pre-season training session.

Rafa had signed Djibril Cissé, a powerful new French striker, and two creative Spanish midfielders, Xabi Alonso and Luis García. Stevie was starting to get excited about the future of Liverpool Football Club.

But as the 2004–05 season was just about to start, Stevie got some bad news. Michael had been quiet for a few weeks and Rafa left him on the bench for the Champions League qualifier.

'What's going on?' Stevie asked. He was worried about his friend and teammate.

Michael couldn't keep the secret any longer. 'Real

Madrid have made a great offer for me and I've decided to go,' he said.

Stevie was very sad to see Michael leave but he knew how much he wanted to play abroad for a big club. 'We'll miss you, mate,' he said, giving Michael a hug. 'I understand – the chance to become a *galactico* is a dream come true. Good luck!'

Michael had been Liverpool's top goalscorer for years. Without him, what would they do? Rafa had a great idea.

'I want Didi and Xabi to play deeper in midfield,' he told Stevie when he called him into his office. 'I have a new role for you – I want you to get into the box and score goals!'

Stevie loved his new role behind the striker. He still did lots of tackling but it was really fun to push forward in attack. He had the energy to make great runs into the penalty area and his shooting got better and better.

'I've never scored more than ten goals in a season,' Stevie told Carra. 'This year, I'm going to beat that easily!'

In the final match of the Champions League group stage in December, Liverpool needed to beat Olympiacos by two goals to go through. Stevie loved playing against the best teams in Europe and he was desperate to stay in the tournament. The atmosphere at Anfield was unbelievable. The fans believed that their team could do it, and that inspired the players.

Olympiacos took the lead but Stevie didn't give up. 'We'll just have to score three!' he told his teammates at half-time.

Florent Sinama Pongolle scored the first Liverpool goal, and with ten minutes to go, Neil Mellor scored the second. 'We only need one more goal, lads. Come on, we can do this!' Stevie shouted. With the captain's armband around his sleeve, it was time to be a leader.

Liverpool played the ball down the left wing but Stevie was in lots of space on the right. 'Over here!' he called with his arms in the air. Eventually, Neil headed the ball back into Stevie's path. This was it – he needed to stay calm and get his technique right. Just outside the penalty area, Stevie struck the ball and it flew through the air and into the corner of the net.

Goooooooooooooooooooooooooaaaaaaaaaaaaaaaaaaa alllllllllllllllllllllllllllllllllllll!!!!!!!!!

Stevie ran towards the fans, pumping his fists. It was a really special moment. At the final whistle, all of the players hugged each other. They still had a long way to go but Stevie was really pleased with the team spirit.

In the semi-final, Liverpool were up against Chelsea, the team that Stevie had nearly signed for. It would be a great feeling to beat them and reach the Champions League final. Ahead of the two games, Stevie and Carra swapped lots of banter with Frank and John about who would win. There was lots of pride at stake.

'We can't lose this, boys!' Stevie told his teammates in the dressing room. 'This is the biggest match of the season. We have to show that we're the best team in England.'

The first leg at Stamford Bridge finished 0–0. It was a good result to take back to Anfield but it wouldn't be easy. The Liverpool fans were louder than ever, singing the names of their star players.

Steve Gerrard, Gerrard
He'll pass the ball forty yards
He shoots the ball really hard
Steve Gerrard, Gerrard

After four minutes, Stevie flicked the ball through to Milan Baroš. The goalkeeper blocked Milan's shot but the ball bounced straight to Luis García. William Gallas blocked his shot but the ball was over the line. Goal! The Chelsea players complained to the referee but Liverpool had taken the lead.

'Stay focused!' Stevie shouted to his teammates as they celebrated.

The Liverpool fans cheered every pass and every tackle. Stevie never stopped running in midfield and Carra played the game of his life in defence. The second half seemed to go on for hours but at last, the referee blew the final whistle. Stevie and Carra hugged and danced around the pitch. Liverpool were in the Champions League final. All of the players partied late into the night.

'This is amazing!' Stevie said as he looked at all of the Liverpool fans at Istanbul airport. The whole city was painted red for the final. AC Milan were the favourites because they had great players like Andrea Pirlo, Kaká and Andriy Shevchenko but Stevie knew that they had a good chance of winning, especially with so much support in the stadium.

'I think the whole of Liverpool is here!' Carra joked as they travelled to the stadium for the game.

None of the players had slept because they were so nervous and excited. Playing in the Champions League final was the biggest match of their lives. In the dressing room, Stevie tried to inspire his team.

'We've done so well to get this far but if we win this, we will go home as heroes,' he shouted and his teammates cheered loudly.

When AC Milan scored in the first minute, the Liverpool players were shocked but Stevie told them to keep calm and carry on. By half-time it was 3–0 and most people thought the game was over, but not Stevie.

'Did you see the Milan players smiling and waving to their families?' he asked his teammates. 'They think they've already won this but they haven't!'

Manager Rafa's team talk was simple: 'Keep your heads up and remember that you play for Liverpool. Believe in yourselves and do it for the thousands of fans out there.'

The players sat and listened to the noise of the supporters. They never stopped singing. Stevie and the others were ready to fight in the second half.

A cross came in from the left and it was perfect for Stevie. He leapt into the air and used his neck muscles to power a header into the back of the net. As he ran back to the halfway line, he urged the fans to make even more noise. 'Come on!'

Two minutes later, Vladimír Šmicer scored Liverpool's second goal and suddenly, they were back in the game. They attacked the goal again and again.

'Be patient – we can do this!' Stevie shouted.

Didi played the ball forward to Milan Baroš,

who flicked it cleverly into the box. Stevie sprinted towards the ball but Gennaro Gattuso fouled him just as he was about to shoot. Penalty! Xabi's spot-kick was saved but he tapped in the rebound. It was 3–3! The score remained the same, even after thirty minutes of extra-time. The exciting final would have to be decided by penalties.

'Who wants to take one?' Rafa asked as the players rested on the grass.

'Me!' said Stevie, Vladimír, Luis, Djibril and John Arne Riise. Stevie would take their fifth penalty.

'Win this match for us!' they said to Jerzy Dudek as he went to take his place in goal.

Stevie stood with his teammates and cheered every goal. When Vladimír made it 3–2, the pressure was on Shevchenko to score. If he missed, Stevie wouldn't even need to take his penalty. Jerzy waved his arms and made the save. Liverpool were the winners! The whole team ran as fast as they could to celebrate with their goalkeeping hero.

Championes, Championes, Olé Olé Olé.

The players danced around the pitch and went

towards the fans in the crowd, who had been so important to the success of Liverpool.

'I told you we would win trophies!' Rafa said to Stevie and they laughed and hugged.

As captain, Stevie still had a big job to do. Lifting the trophy was the best feeling ever. Clouds of red smoke flew into the air and the players roared.

Liverpool, Champions of Europe. Stevie was on top of the world.

CHAPTER 17

THE GERRARD FINAL

'How many goals did you get last season?' Paul Jr asked his brother as the family relaxed at home in Huyton over the summer. Even when Stevie wasn't playing football, they usually still talked about it. After all, they were both Liverpool fans and they were looking forward to the next season.

'Thirteen in all competitions,' he replied. 'It's my best yet but I can do better.'

'Do you think you can score twenty?' Paul Jr asked. He knew how much his brother loved a challenge.

'Sure, why not?' Stevie laughed.

Stevie was a key goalscorer for the team now and

he enjoyed the responsibility. Whenever he could, he rushed forward to get in good positions for shooting. Liverpool were chasing Manchester United at the top of the Premiership but they truly excelled in cup competitions. They thrashed Birmingham 7–0 in the FA Cup quarter-final and then beat Chelsea 2–1 in the semi-final.

'Another trip to the Millennium Stadium!' Stevie joked with Carra as they celebrated the victory.

The final, held in Cardiff in May 2006, would be the last match of an excellent season for Stevie. Liverpool finished third behind Chelsea and Manchester United in the league, but he won the PFA Players' Player of the Year and there was still one last chance to win a trophy.

'There's no such thing as an easy final, boys,' he told them in the dressing room. 'And there's no such thing as favourites. If we don't play well, we will lose. Let's make this *our* FA Cup final!'

Their FA Cup Final opponents, West Ham, started really well and after half an hour they were leading 2–0.

'Come on boys!' Stevie shouted. 'We're half asleep – we need to get going in this game!'

Stevie got the ball deep in midfield and looked up. They needed him to do something special. Djibril was making a run behind the West Ham defence. It was the kind of long-range pass that Stevie loved to play. The ball landed right at Djibril's feet and he volleyed it powerfully into the net. Thanks to their captain, Liverpool were back in contention.

'This is like Istanbul all over again!' Djibril joked. 'Let's get another goal.'

West Ham defended well but Stevie knew he just needed to get into the right areas to score. When Peter Crouch headed the ball down to the edge of the penalty area, Stevie was there waiting. Instead of calmly placing the ball in the corner, he smashed it into the top corner.

'Game on!' Stevie shouted as he ran back for kick-off.

They were flying but out of the blue, West Ham took the lead again. Liverpool attacked relentlessly but they couldn't find another goal. On this hot

May afternoon, the players were tired and time was running out.

Rafa brought on Didi and shouted instructions to Stevie. 'Push forward!'

In injury time, the ball fell to Stevie. He was over thirty yards from goal and his legs felt heavy but he knew that it would take something spectacular to take the game into extra time. He was having a brilliant match – what did he have to lose?

As soon as the ball left his foot, Stevie knew he had hit it perfectly. He watched as it travelled like an arrow past all of the defenders and into the bottom corner.

Goooooooooooooooooooooaaaaaaaaaaaaaaaaaaaaaaaa allllllllllllllllllllllllll!!!!!!!!!!!!!!!

Stevie had saved the day yet again for his team. The adrenaline was rushing through his body. He had just become the first player ever to score in FA Cup, League Cup, UEFA Cup and Champions League finals. As he celebrated next to the fans, he pointed to the name on his back: 'GERRARD'. With every important goal, he became more of a Liverpool legend.

Both teams struggled through extra time. Penalties would decide the final again.

'I'm ready to take one!' Stevie told Rafa. As captain, he needed to lead by example.

Stevie sent Shaka Hislop the wrong way to make it 3–1. John Arne scored and when Pepe Reina saved Anton Ferdinand's penalty, the match was over. The whole team ran to celebrate with Pepe but Stevie was the real hero.

'They'll call that "The Gerrard Final",' Carra said as they jogged around the pitch, clapping and waving to the fans. Stevie loved the sound of that.

CHAPTER 18

WORLD CUP HEARTBREAK

It had been a long and exhausting club season but in the summer of 2006, Stevie and Carra were excited to represent their country in the biggest tournament in the world. For the World Cup, staged in Germany, most of the players from Euro 2004 were in the squad again and there were great expectations for England's 'golden generation'.

'Paraguay, Trinidad and Tobago, and then Sweden,' Stevie said, looking at the schedule. 'We can do this!'

England won their first two games and Stevie scored a great goal against Trinidad and Tobago with his left foot. Confidence was really high in the camp,

especially with Wayne Rooney returning from injury.
Manager Sven-Göran Eriksson rested Stevie for the
final group match against Sweden but even then, he
came off the bench and scored a header to force a
draw. Stevie felt unstoppable.

In the second round, Beckham scored a free-
kick to beat Ecuador and set up a re-match against
Portugal. Stevie couldn't wait for revenge.

'We'll beat them this time!' he said and they all
believed it.

It was a very tight match and the Portuguese
defenders kept fouling Wayne. Everywhere he went,
they pulled his shirt and kicked his ankles. Stevie
could see that his teammate was getting frustrated.

'Stay calm and we'll score,' he told him. 'Don't let
it get to you.'

The referee blew the whistle and Stevie thought it
was just another free-kick to England. But the referee
gave Wayne a red card! He couldn't believe it.

'Ref, what did he do?' Stevie asked.

'He stamped on the defender,' he replied.

Stevie knew Wayne well and there was no way

that he would have done that on purpose. It must have been an accident.

'Come on lads, we just have to keep going,' Stevie said, trying to lift his teammates' spirits. They were angry about the sending off but they were even more determined to win.

The match was still 0–0 after 120 minutes. It was time for penalties yet again and Stevie was ready to play his part.

'This time, we have to win this,' he told his teammates. They couldn't lose to Portugal on penalties twice.

Simão Sabrosa scored but Frank's shot was saved. Portugal had the advantage. Stevie stood on the halfway line with his teammates and waited for his turn.

It felt like such a long walk to the penalty spot but Stevie took deep breaths and tried to stay focused on scoring. He took penalties all the time and his country was relying on him. He was ready but the referee took ages to blow his whistle. Suddenly, Stevie started to doubt himself. There was so much pressure on him, both in the stadium and back home in England.

Stevie ran up and kicked it towards the bottom corner but he knew he hadn't got it right. The goalkeeper guessed where it would go and made the save. With his head down, Stevie walked slowly back to the halfway line. He couldn't look at his teammates; he had let them down badly. At Liverpool and in training, he scored every time. What had gone wrong?

England were knocked out and Stevie sat down in the centre-circle with tears in his eyes. It was the worst feeling in the world. He tried to think ahead to the prospect of winning more trophies but the defeat was really hard to accept. It had been one of England's best chances to win a World Cup since that summer of 1966, forty years earlier.

'It's time to move on, son,' Paul Sr said when Stevie returned to Liverpool. 'Remember, you'll have more chances to win that trophy.'

CHAPTER 19

DEADLY DUO PART I: STEVIE & FERNANDO

'Fernando Torres!' Stevie said excitedly. His brother had called him while he was relaxing by the pool on holiday. He had some big transfer news. 'Are you sure?'

'Yes, we've just signed him for £26.5 million,' Paul Jr replied. 'He's exactly the kind of world-class player that you need around you.'

'Finally, we've got someone else to score some goals!' Stevie joked.

He was really pleased to hear that the club would have a new superstar striker. It was a few years since the glory days when Robbie Fowler and Michael Owen would each score twenty goals a season. Stevie had seen Fernando play lots of times for

Atlético Madrid and Spain. He was one of the best young strikers in Europe.

'Welcome to Liverpool,' Stevie said to Fernando, shaking his hand as he arrived for pre-season training.

Fernando was quick, clever, and a brilliant finisher. The one doubt that people had about him was whether or not he was strong enough for the Premier League. The defending was much more physical than in La Liga, and he looked skinny. Stevie knew there was only one way to find out.

'When he first gets the ball, give him the biggest tackle you've got,' he whispered to Carra. Carra smiled; he loved a big tackle.

Fernando fell to the floor but he didn't complain. He got back to his feet and looked for the ball again. When Stevie passed it to him, he flicked it past Carra before he could even try to stop him. Fernando ran through and shot the ball into the bottom corner.

Carra looked at Stevie and nodded – Fernando was definitely strong enough for the Premier League. He had the determination of a top striker.

'I've got a good feeling about this partnership,' Stevie said to Fernando as they walked off the training pitch. 'The Premier League better watch out!'

The more they played together, the better they understood each other. When Stevie got the ball in midfield, he always knew where Fernando was and where he would move next. Everything was so easy. They didn't need to talk about it; they could read each other's minds. With Fernando holding the ball up, Stevie was scoring more goals than ever.

In April 2008, against Blackburn Rovers, Stevie made his 300th appearance for Liverpool in the Premier League.

'Are you really only twenty-seven?' one of the younger players joked with him. 'You've been around for ages!'

'Don't be so cheeky,' he replied, giving a friendly slap. 'I'll be around for plenty more years, especially when our youngsters are so rubbish!'

During the Blackburn game, Stevie ran forward with the ball. There were lots of defenders around him but he could see Fernando in space. He passed and then kept moving towards goal. Fernando flicked the ball through for the one-two and Stevie placed the ball past the goalkeeper. 1–0!

In the second half, Stevie received the ball on the right wing. Without even thinking, he crossed it towards the back post. Fernando slipped away from his marker and headed the ball down into the bottom corner. 2–0! It was Fernando's thirtieth goal of the season and Stevie wasn't far behind him.

'You're unstoppable!' Rafa said at the final whistle, with one arm around each of his superstars. With Stevie and Fernando, they really could win the Premiership.

As they went into their final game of 2008 against Newcastle, Liverpool were top of the league and Stevie believed that they could go all the way. With Fernando injured, he needed to keep scoring. Stevie got the first and the fourth goals as Liverpool won 5–1.

'We just have to keep doing what we're doing,' he told his teammates after the match. 'We're the best team in England right now but there's still half a season to go.'

Liverpool struggled in January and February and

suddenly Manchester United were back at the top of the table. Stevie wasn't happy. He was so competitive and he hated to see the team throwing everything away.

'It's no good beating Chelsea but then losing to Middlesbrough,' he shouted angrily, throwing his shinpads to the dressing-room floor. 'We have to stay focused in every game!'

By March, Fernando was fully fit again, just in time for a massive month. First up, they played Real Madrid in the Champions League. Stevie loved playing against the top European clubs and he knew that they had a great chance of winning.

'If we get an early goal, they won't know what's hit them,' he told Carra as they got ready to run out at Anfield. They could hear the incredible noise of the crowd, like it was a twelfth player for Liverpool.

Fernando scored the early goal and Stevie made it 2–0 from the penalty spot. At half-time, it was all looking good but Stevie refused to relax.

'We can't switch off, boys. We've got forty-five minutes to go!'

Two minutes into the second half, Ryan Babel

crossed from the left and Stevie made his trademark run to the penalty spot. As the ball arrived, he smashed it into the top of net.

Goooooooooooooooooooooooaaaaaaaaaaaaaaaaalllll llllllllllllllllllllllllllllll!!!!!!!!!!!!

The Kop went wild as Stevie ran past with his arms outstretched. The fans loved big European nights and this was one of the biggest.

The game finished 4–0 but after a short celebration, it was back to the Premier League and another very important match, against title rivals Manchester United.

'I don't think I've ever wanted to win a game more,' Stevie told his dad the night before. He was so excited that he couldn't sleep. 'If I don't score, I know Fernando will and vice versa. This is the best team I've played with. We have to win this!'

Even when United took the lead, Stevie didn't stop believing. Five minutes later, Fernando broke free and equalised.

'That's it – come on boys!' Stevie shouted, pumping his fists.

Just before half-time, Fernando spotted Stevie's run down the right. His pass was perfect but just as Stevie got to it, Patrice Evra fouled him. Penalty! Stevie placed it perfectly into the bottom corner. He was so happy to score that he kissed the Liverpool badge on his shirt and then the TV camera lens.

Liverpool defended really well and in the last fifteen minutes, they scored two more goals.

'4–1 – we destroyed them!' Stevie cheered at the final whistle, as he hugged Carra. He was so proud of his team's performance and now they were right back in the title race, four points behind with nine games to go.

Under Stevie's leadership, Liverpool kept winning. He even scored his first ever hat-trick against Aston Villa but unfortunately, Manchester United kept winning too. At the end of the season, Liverpool were still four points behind. It was really disappointing to come so close to winning the league but they had given everything.

'Well done, lads,' Stevie said, patting everyone on the back. 'This time, we finished second. Next time, we'll finish first!'

CHAPTER 20

CAPTAIN OF ENGLAND

'His record is amazing – AC Milan, Real Madrid, Roma, Juventus.'

'I hear he has really strict rules. He looks scary!'

The England players were excited about their new manager, Fabio Capello. Some of them were worried that he would be too cold and tough but Stevie loved hard work and discipline. It's what the team needed in order to succeed in a major tournament.

'Stevie, you're one of my three key senior players,' Fabio told him at the first training camp. 'You, John Terry and Rio Ferdinand will be my captains on the pitch.'

Stevie was pleased to hear that. Capello's style

was very similar to Rafa's at Liverpool. He was very professional and focused on qualifying for the 2010 World Cup. To get there, John would be the official leader and Stevie would be his second-in-command.

In November 2007, a defeat to Croatia meant that England didn't make it to the European Championships in Austria and Switzerland. Within a year, after seven wins in a row, England faced Croatia again – this time in order to secure World Cup qualification – and they needed revenge.

'We're in great form, lads,' John told his teammates in the dressing room before kick-off. 'We've got nothing to fear. Let's go out there and show them how far we've come in the last year.'

England were so determined to win. In the first ten minutes, Frank scored a penalty and after that, they were unstoppable. Stevie spread the ball wide to Aaron Lennon and ran towards the back post. Aaron's cross was perfect and Stevie powered his header into the far corner of the net. He pumped his fists and high-fived his teammates.

'Come on, let's thrash them!' Stevie shouted.

In the second half, Frank scored again and then
Wayne flicked a ball back towards the penalty spot. He
knew that Stevie would be there and he headed the
ball into the roof of the net. 4–0! Stevie slid towards
the corner flag on his knees. In front of 80,000 England
fans, they were playing some brilliant football. There
was a party atmosphere at Wembley. Everyone was
looking forward to the big tournament in South Africa.

Capello made Rio Ferdinand his new captain
but just one week before the World Cup began,
he picked up an injury at a training session. So the
England manager called Stevie into his office.

'Congratulations, you'll be our captain for the
tournament,' Capello said. 'I need you to lead by
example, just like you do at Liverpool.'

Stevie nodded with a big smile on his face.
Captaining his country at a World Cup was a dream
come true. He would do everything to make his
nation proud.

In the first match against the USA, Stevie made a
great run forward in attack. Emile Heskey saw it and
cleverly flicked the ball through. In the penalty area,

Stevie poked the ball past the goalkeeper with the outside of his right foot.

Goooooooooooooooooooaaaaaaaaaaaaaaaallllllllllllllll llllllllllllllll!!!!!!!!!!!!!!!!!!!!!

England were off to a great start and the whole team celebrated together. They were in control of the game until Clint Dempsey took a long-range shot. There wasn't much power on it but as Rob Green went to catch the ball, it slipped through his fingers and into the goal. It was a bad mistake but Stevie needed his players to keep going.

'Forget about that, lads,' he shouted, clapping to encourage his teammates. 'We've got plenty of time to score another goal.'

England couldn't get a winner but a draw wasn't a bad first result. After a boring 0–0 draw against Algeria, England had to beat Slovenia to go through to the second round. Stevie was playing on the right of midfield, instead of his preferred role in the middle. It wasn't his favourite position but he would play anywhere to help his country. It was such a relief when Jermain Defoe scored the crucial goal.

'We need to do much better,' Stevie told his teammates, 'but at least we're through!'

Next up were England's biggest rivals, Germany. Stevie knew they would have to play the game of their lives to win. Germany took the lead after twenty minutes but England didn't give up. At 2–1, Frank hit a great shot that smacked the crossbar and bounced down over the goal line. The players started to celebrate but the linesman said that the ball hadn't crossed the line.

'That should have been a goal!' Stevie shouted to the referee. 'Even I could see that it went over the line.'

It was no use; in the end, Germany were just too skilful. They scored four goals, two of them by Thomas Müller, and England were knocked out of the World Cup. It was another disappointing tournament for their 'golden generation'.

'We did our best but it wasn't good enough,' Stevie said to Wayne as they slowly left the pitch in Bloemfontein.

He loved being the England captain but time was really running out for Stevie to win an international trophy.

CHAPTER 21

GETTING OLDER

'You're getting older, son,' Paul Sr reminded Stevie as he rested his leg in front of the TV. 'You have to take more care of yourself now. You can't rush about the pitch flying into tackles all the time like you used to.'

Stevie had injured his Achilles tendon and he hated not playing football. Liverpool were struggling in mid-table and there was nothing that he could do to help. He was used to playing through pain but this time he had to take a break.

'If you keep playing, you'll do even more damage,' the Liverpool physio Chris Morgan warned him. 'You have to rest!'

Stevie didn't want his career to end at thirty and

so he did as he was told. With more than a month on the sidelines, it took him a while to get back to full fitness. After Xabi Alonso had gone to Real Madrid, Stevie was playing a deeper midfield role again. But just as he was finding his form once more, he suffered another injury – this time, much worse.

As he did a Cruyff Turn in a training match at Melwood, Stevie felt an intense pain in his upper leg. He had had groin problems for years but this felt serious. Stevie hobbled off the field and went straight to the physio.

'You've got two options,' Chris explained to him as he lay on the treatment table. 'Either you can have surgery now and be out for a few months, or you can see if it heals itself.'

'If we do nothing, there's a good chance that you could lose a lot of power when you kick the ball,' the surgeon told him.

Stevie thought about his favourite cross-field passes and his long-range shooting. There was no way that he could risk losing his power. 'Let's do the surgery,' he said.

'Good choice,' the surgeon said with a confident smile. 'Frank had the same operation and he was back playing again within three months.'

It was the end of Stevie's season but hopefully he'd be raring to go for pre-season in July. The surgery was successful and he had a great new scar to show off. But as Stevie began doing his strengthening exercises, he was still in a lot of pain.

'Okay, you need to rest for a bit longer,' Chris told him, as he checked the injury. 'Be patient – it still needs time to heal.'

Patience wasn't one of Stevie's strengths. When he went on holiday to Portugal with his wife Alex and the kids, he asked Chris to go too. In the afternoons, the family relaxed in the sun but in the mornings and evenings, Stevie worked hard in the gym.

'Do you think I'll be ready for July?' he asked. The exercises still hurt but it was getting better.

'Let's keep our fingers crossed and wait and see,' Chris replied. The worst thing they could do was to rush Stevie's recovery.

In the end it was September before Stevie could

play again. He was so happy as he came on as a substitute after six months out.

'I'm back!' Stevie said to himself. He had missed football so much.

By the time that Manchester United came to Anfield in October 2011, he was back to full fitness. As Stevie led his team out on to the pitch, there was a really serious look on his face. Liverpool needed a victory and he was determined to be the hero.

In the middle of the second half, they won a free-kick just outside the Manchester United penalty area. Charlie Adam picked up the ball to take it, and Stewart Downing was there too. They were both very good at free-kicks but Stevie didn't care.

'I've got this one,' he said. He was in the mood to score.

Stevie struck the ball low and hard into the bottom corner. The Manchester United goalkeeper didn't even move. Stevie felt so much joy that he thought his chest might explode. It felt so good to be back to his best for Liverpool. As the fans went wild in the Kop, Stevie ran straight towards them, pointing. He slid along the grass on his knees and kissed the club badge on his shirt.

After such an emotional game, the slight pain in his ankle didn't seem like anything to worry about. But as Stevie walked along the Anfield corridors, Chris saw him and he saw the swollen ankle. They rushed Stevie to hospital and caught the infection just in time. But Stevie didn't feel lucky; he just felt really low.

'Chris, I'm thirty-one years old and I think it's the end for me,' he said. He couldn't look his physio and friend in the eyes.

Chris took him to see Steve Peters, a renowned sports psychiatrist. Stevie was nervous as he arrived on crutches but they talked and talked about how he was feeling.

'What is your biggest worry?' Steve asked.

'Not being able to play football again,' Stevie said immediately.

'Are you happy at home?' Steve continued. He wasn't scared to ask personal questions.

'Yes, my family are amazing. I have a wonderful wife and three beautiful daughters.'

'Is that more important to you than football?'

Stevie nodded. 'Of course.'

'You need to stop worrying about your career,' Steve told him at the end of their first meeting. 'I've spoken to your doctors and they have no doubts that you'll be back. You have to focus your mind back on to your family and the trophies you've already won.'

It all made sense and with Steve's help, Stevie started to get back to his old, confident self. He had three or four years left as a footballer and, with a new hero in the Liverpool squad, Stevie was determined to make the most of that time.

CHAPTER 22

DEADLY DUO PART II:
STEVIE & LUIS

'Welcome to Liverpool,' Stevie said to Luis Suárez as
he arrived at Melwood for his first training session.
Fernando had signed for Chelsea and the club
needed a new star striker. Luis cost £23 million after
scoring numerous goals in Holland. But how would
the Uruguayan enjoy rainy mornings in England?

Carra was ready to test Luis just as he had tested
Fernando back in 2007.

'The Dutch league is nothing compared to the
Premier League,' Carra said. 'We need to see if he's
ready to step up to the next level.'

Even at a five-a-side practice match Luis ran
around like it was a cup final. He was everywhere,

calling for the ball and then dribbling past defenders and scoring goals. When the other team had the ball, he never stopped fighting and chasing. He didn't give the defenders a single second to think. Liverpool definitely had a new superstar.

'He's the most annoying striker I've ever played against,' Carra complained as they left the field. He was exhausted and embarrassed. 'I think he's even better than Fernando!'

Stevie couldn't wait to see Luis play in a proper match. He liked being one of the best players at Liverpool but world-class teammates always brought the best out of him. To match Luis's talents, Stevie worked harder than ever. He wasn't as quick as he used to be but he still had the experience and vision to play great passes, especially when he had strikers ahead of him making such clever runs.

In the League Cup Final in February 2012, Liverpool were up against Cardiff City – a particularly big game for Stevie and his family.

'Looking forward to Wembley?' Stevie texted his cousin, Anthony. After starting at Everton, Anthony

Gerrard was now Cardiff's centre-back. They couldn't wait to play against each other.

'Of course! The underdogs are ready for a shock win,' Anthony texted back.

'I have family pride resting on this game,' Stevie told his teammates in the dressing room before kick-off. 'If we go into this match thinking it'll be easy, they'll beat us. Let's give it everything and win another trophy!'

Cardiff scored first but in the second half Luis headed the ball towards goal and it hit the post. The ball bounced to Martin Škrtel and he scored the rebound. In extra time, Liverpool had lots of chances to score and finally, Dirk Kuyt put the ball in the net. Stevie thought they'd won it but Cardiff equalised right at the end. It was time for another penalty shoot-out.

With his teammates standing together on the halfway line, Stevie made the long walk to take the first penalty. He placed the ball on the spot and as he walked back for his run-up, he focused on where he would place his shot. He aimed for the top left corner but it didn't quite go high enough and the goalkeeper made a great save to tip it onto the crossbar and over. Stevie slowly moved back to his teammates with his hands on his head. They patted him on the back and told him not to worry, but Stevie hated to let his team down.

Charlie hit Liverpool's second penalty over the bar and suddenly they were in real trouble. Luckily, Dirk, Stewart Downing and Glen Johnson all scored and it came down to Cardiff's fifth taker – Stevie's cousin Anthony. Anthony hit a low shot but it went wide of the post. Liverpool were the winners.

Stevie felt really sorry for Anthony but his teammates were piling on top of their goalkeeper, Pepe Reina, and he ran to join in. After more than a year of injury problems, it was a great feeling to walk up the steps and have a winner's medal placed around his neck. As Stevie raised the trophy into the air, the Liverpool fans cheered wildly.

'Congratulations on your first English trophy!' Stevie said to Luis. 'Are you happy?'

Luis smiled. 'I'm very happy but this is just the start. I want to win many more.'

Stevie loved Luis's ambition; it was exactly what

Liverpool needed to become a better team. Like Stevie, Luis hated losing more than anything in the world. Together, they were forming a great partnership in attack. Luis was a great goalscorer but he was also very good at creating goals for others.

In the Merseyside derby against Everton, the ball came to Stevie on the edge of the area. The goalkeeper was off his line and so Stevie calmly lifted the ball into the back of the net with his left foot.

Goooooooooooooooooooaaaaaaaaaaaaaaaaaaaaaaaaall !!

Early in the second half, Luis cut inside from the right wing. He nutmegged one defender and then dribbled past a second. He was nearly in a position to shoot but he saw Stevie running forward. As he arrived, Luis stepped back and Stevie smashed the ball into the net.

Stevie ran to the fans, holding up two fingers for two goals. Then he looked around for Luis and when he came running over, he gave him a big hug.

'Thanks, what a run!' Stevie shouted over the noise of the celebrating Liverpool fans.

A hat-trick against their local rivals would be one of the best moments of Stevie's career, and he was desperate to score one more goal. In injury time, an Everton midfielder slipped and Stevie dribbled forward. Luis ran to the left and Stevie passed to him. Two defenders closed Luis down and so he cut inside and passed back to Stevie, who was now in lots of space. Stevie put the ball in the net and pointed to Luis with a huge smile on his face.

'You're the best!' Stevie said as they hugged again.

In his first full Premier League season for Liverpool, Luis scored twenty-three goals. Every time he got the ball in attack, he looked dangerous. Defenders backed away, or tried to foul him, but Luis was unstoppable. All he needed was more support and Liverpool made two more formidable attacking signings: Daniel Sturridge from Chelsea and Philippe Coutinho from Inter Milan.

As Stevie watched the skill and speed of Luis, Daniel and Philippe, he got really excited. 'Next season, I really believe that we can win the league!'

CHAPTER 23

THE SLIP

'They're calling us "SAS"!' Daniel Sturridge said after another great victory. In a 4–1 win over West Brom, Luis Suárez had scored three and Daniel had scored one. There was a fun rivalry between the two of them about who could score the most goals.

'There should be a third "S" in that!' Raheem Sterling added. The young winger's pace and trickery was causing lots of problems for Premier League defences.

'And a "C"!' Philippe Coutinho added.

'And a "G"!' Stevie Gerrard said and everyone nodded. Their captain was their leader. In his deeper midfield role, he was the one that started every move with his brilliant passing. Stevie's experience was so important with lots of young players in the side.

On Christmas Day 2013, Liverpool were top of the Premier League but after defeats to Manchester City and Chelsea the following week, they slipped down to fifth.

'We're playing so well against the lower teams,' Stevie said to his teammates at the start of 2014, 'but we have to do better in the big games.'

The first big test of the new year was Arsenal. The Liverpool manager at the time, Brendan Rodgers, told his players to start strongly. 'I want us to attack as much as possible in the first fifteen minutes. If we run at the Arsenal defence with our pace and movement, they won't be able to handle it. And once we get one goal, we'll get many!'

They certainly listened to their manager's instructions. In the first minute, Stevie curled a great free-kick into the box and Martin tapped it in.

'That's it!' Stevie shouted as they celebrated. 'Let's keep going – they'll be nervous now, so let's score a few more.'

Stevie was the creator again, as Martin scored
a brilliant header from his corner kick. Then Luis
played the ball across the penalty area and Raheem
made it 3–0. Liverpool were just too good for Arsenal
and the match finished 5–1.

'What a performance!' Stevie said at the final
whistle as he went round high-fiving all of his
teammates. 'Thirteen more games like that and we'll
be Premier League champions!'

After three wins in a row, Liverpool were now
back at second place in the Premiership. When
they went to Old Trafford, the squad were full
of confidence, and Stevie had no doubt that
they could win. In the crowd, the Liverpool fans
showed off a huge new banner that said 'MAKE
US DREAM'.

After fifteen minutes, Daniel crossed to Luis at
the back post. As he controlled the ball and tried to
play it past the defender, it struck his arm. Handball!
Penalty! Stevie had missed a few important penalties
during his career but he never stopped believing
that he could score. He placed the ball carefully on

the spot and then waited with his hands on his hips. When the referee blew the whistle, Stevie sent the goalkeeper the wrong way and put his shot right in the corner of the net.

'That's a perfect penalty!' Raheem said to Stevie, giving him a big hug.

He loved scoring against Manchester United and the fans knew how much it meant to him.

Steve Gerrard, Gerrard
He'll pass the ball forty yards
He shoots the ball really hard
Steve Gerrard, Gerrard

At the start of the second half, Liverpool won another penalty. As Stevie stepped up to take it, the fans wondered where he would put his second spot-kick of the match – in the same corner as the last one, or in the opposite corner? Stevie knew exactly what he was doing and even though the goalkeeper went the right way this time, his shot was right in the corner.

Stevie ran and did his trademark knee-slide along the grass. He was so happy to play a big part in Liverpool's best title challenge in years. The whole team huddled together to show just how strong they were. In the last few minutes, Luis made it 3–0.

'We can do this!' Stevie shouted in the dressing room after the game and his teammates cheered loudly.

Four more wins later, Liverpool were top of the league with five games to go. They were close but they still had two massive matches left – Manchester City and then Chelsea.

It was an emotional day as Stevie led his team out on to the pitch for the first of these matches. It was now twenty-five years since the Hillsborough disaster. Stevie touched the 'This is Anfield' sign and thought of his cousin Jon-Paul. He would be so proud of how well Liverpool were doing. As the minute's silence ended, 40,000 Liverpool supporters roared around the stadium – it was game time.

'Come on, we're ready for this!' Stevie screamed to his teammates.

Raheem made a great run from the left to the right. Luis's pass was perfect and he controlled the ball, tricked a defender and then put the ball in the net. It was a dream start and the whole team piled on top of Raheem. Then from a Stevie corner, Martin Škrtel scored another header. He slid on his knees towards Stevie and they hugged and rolled around the grass. They felt unstoppable.

But in the second half, Manchester City scored two quick goals and suddenly the pressure was on Liverpool to find a winner. Stevie's head went down for a second but he quickly got back to urging his team to attack.

'Keep going, get forward!' he yelled.

City had lots of chances to score again but Liverpool refused to give up. Players like Stevie and Luis had brought a winning mentality to the team. A clearance fell to Philippe Coutinho on the edge of the penalty area and he curled the ball first time into the bottom corner.

Goooooooooooooooooooooooaaaaaaaaaaaaaaaaaaaaaaaa llllllllllllllllllllllllllllllllllll!!!!!!!!!

At the final whistle, Stevie gathered his players together in a huddle. 'This isn't over yet,' he told them. 'This does not slip now! This does not slip!'

The players cheered and turned to clap the fans, who were singing 'We're going to win the league'. Liverpool were still on track to win the title for the first time in twenty-four years. First, however, they had to beat Norwich, Chelsea, Crystal Palace and Newcastle.

The Chelsea match was the biggest match of Stevie's career. After fifteen years in the Liverpool first team, he had an amazing opportunity to win the Premiership, the best league in the world.

Chelsea's manager José Mourinho knew all about Liverpool's quick starts and so he slowed the game down as much as possible. Liverpool didn't have many chances and they grew more and more frustrated.

In the last minute of the first half, Stevie came deeper into defence to get the ball. Demba Ba, the Chelsea striker, rushed to close him down. The ball slipped under Stevie's foot and as he ran to get it back, he fell to the floor. He was in trouble. Ba ran through and scored past the goalkeeper. It was a big mistake but the Liverpool fans were supportive.

Stevie Gerrard is our captain
Stevie Gerrard is a red
Stevie Gerrard plays for Liverpool
A Scouser born and bred

In the dressing room, Liverpool manager Brendan Rodgers tried to lift the spirits of his players. 'We need to stay calm. It's only 1–0 and we have plenty of time. You're trying too hard.'

Stevie was desperate to make up for his error in the second half but the Chelsea defence was too good. It was the worst moment of his career as Stevie walked off down the tunnel. Liverpool had lost and it was his fault.

'Remember all of the amazing things that you've done for the club,' Rodgers said as tears streamed down Stevie's face. 'Remember all of the trophies that you've won, and remember that incredible night in Istanbul. You're a Liverpool legend and they'll never forget that.'

Against Crystal Palace, Liverpool were 3–0 up. Stevie was feeling a bit better after helping to set up two of the goals.

'Come on, we can still beat Manchester City to the title!' Stevie shouted as they celebrated.

But in the last ten minutes, it all went wrong. Crystal Palace scored one, then another and then another. It was 3–3 and they couldn't believe what had happened. At the final whistle, Luis lifted his shirt over his face and cried and cried. They had all worked so hard and they had got so close to winning the league. It was a terrible feeling. Stevie helped Luis to his feet. He pushed the TV cameras away and walked with his teammate off the pitch.

'We did our best,' Stevie said. 'We should all be very proud.'

CHAPTER 24

THE END

'I feel so old!' Stevie said as he lay down on the treatment table while Chris massaged his back. He howled in pain; his whole body ached. It was getting harder and harder to play ninety minutes of fast Premier League football.

'Well it's a good thing that you're off for a holiday in the USA then,' Chris replied with a cheeky smile on his face. He would miss his favourite Liverpool player.

After months of thought, Stevie had decided to follow David Beckham and Frank Lampard by concluding his career as a player in the American MLS (Major League Soccer). It was the most difficult decision he had ever made and as his big farewell got nearer and nearer, he wondered if he was making a mistake.

'Are you sure you want to go? LA is very different to Liverpool!' his brother Paul Jr kept asking.

'Don't leave – we still need you!' his teammates told him.

But as he limped from the physio room to his car, Stevie knew that it was time to move on. He had played seventeen amazing seasons in the Liverpool shirt but he was ready to let the club's new generation of footballers take over.

Stevie's last game at Anfield was an unforgettable day. As he walked out on to the pitch with his daughters, the fans held up cards that spelt out 'SG8' and 'CAPTAIN'. Stevie tried really hard not to cry as he listened to a stadium full of fans singing his name. They had shared so many incredible victories together – the Champions League Final in Istanbul, the FA Cup Final in Cardiff – and he would miss them so much. It was really hard to leave his beloved club.

'Skipper, we've got something for you,' Jordan Henderson said, holding out a book as the team ate dinner together.

The players had collected nice messages from lots of Stevie's teammates, managers and opponents: Robbie Fowler, Fernando Torres, Luis Suárez, Kenny Dalglish, Brendan Rodgers, even Zinedine Zidane.

'Wow!' Stevie couldn't believe it – it was the best gift that he had ever received.

As he read through the pages, his head was full of happy memories. There had been so many highs and lows over the years, but Stevie had loved every minute of his career for Liverpool and England. What an adventure it had been. Through hard work and the support of family, friends and coaches, the skinny local lad had become a Liverpool captain and legend.

Liverpool

- 🏆 FA Cup: 2000–01, 2005–06
- 🏆 League Cup: 2000–01, 2002–03, 2011–12
- 🏆 UEFA Cup: 2000-01
- 🏆 UEFA Super Cup: 2001 UEFA Champions League: 2004–05

Individual

- 🏆 PFA Young Player of the Year: 2001
- 🏆 PFA Team of the Season: 2001, 2004, 2005, 2006, 2007, 2008, 2009, 2014
- 🏆 Ballon d'Or Bronze Award: 2005
- 🏆 UEFA Club Footballer of the Year: 2005
- 🏆 UEFA Team of the Year: 2005, 2006, 2007
- 🏆 FWA Footballer of the Year: 2009

GERRARD

8 THE FACTS

NAME:
Steven George Gerrard

DATE OF BIRTH:
30 May 1980

AGE: 39

PLACE OF BIRTH:
Whiston, Merseyside

NATIONALITY: English

BEST FRIEND: Michael Owen

MAIN CLUB: Liverpool

POSITION: CM

THE STATS

Height (cm):	**183**
Club appearances:	**749**
Club goals:	**191**
Club trophies:	**9**
International appearances:	**114**
International goals:	**21**
International trophies:	**0**
Ballon d'Ors:	**0**

★ ★ ★ **HERO RATING: 89** ★ ★ ★

GREATEST MOMENTS

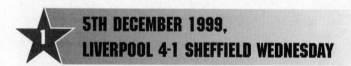

1 — 5TH DECEMBER 1999, LIVERPOOL 4-1 SHEFFIELD WEDNESDAY

1999-2000 season was Stevie's breakthrough season. He was playing well but he hadn't scored yet. That all changed against Sheffield Wednesday. He picked the ball up in central midfield and dribbled forward, past one tackle and then another. Then in the penalty area, he shot powerfully into the bottom corner. What a goal!

1ST SEPTEMBER 2001, GERMANY 1-5 ENGLAND

This was one of England's greatest ever performances and Stevie played a key role. The score was 1-1 when the ball came to him, 30 yards from goal. Stevie chested the ball down and smashed the ball straight into the net. What a way to score your first international goal!

25TH MAY 2005, LIVERPOOL 3-3 AC MILAN (3-2 ON PENALTIES)

This was the famous night that Captain Fantastic led Liverpool to European glory. They were losing 3-0 at half-time in the Champions League final but Stevie didn't give up. He began the best comeback ever with an incredible header and then won the penalty to make it 3-3. This was Stevie's greatest football moment.

4 13TH MAY 2006, LIVERPOOL 3-3 WEST HAM (3-1 ON PENALTIES)

In the 2006 FA Cup Final, Stevie was Liverpool's hero yet again. This time, they were 2-0 down. Stevie hit an unstoppable shot to make it 2-2 but with seconds to go, Liverpool were losing 3-2. He stepped up again with a 35-yard screamer that flew straight past the goalkeeper. Stevie even scored in the penalty shoot-out – it really was the Gerrard Final!

5 16TH MARCH 2014, MANCHESTER UNITED 0-3 LIVERPOOL

In the 2013-14 season, Liverpool got very close to winning their first ever Premier League title. This, a key victory away at massive rivals Manchester United, was Stevie's highlight. He scored two penalties and nearly got his hat-trick! Unfortunately, 6 weeks later, Stevie slipped…

PLAY LIKE YOUR HEROES

THE STEVEN GERRARD CAPTAIN'S COMEBACK

STEP 1: Drop deep to take control of the ball. Look to find your attackers with amazing long-range passes.

STEP 2: When the chance comes, get forward into the penalty area and score a header to get your team back into the game.

STEP 3: As you run back for the kick-off, throw your arms up and down to get the fans cheering even louder.

STEP 4: Put in lots of big tackles to show everyone that you mean business. It's not over yet!

STEP 5: If the space opens up, try one of your trademark long-range shots. They often go in.

STEP 6: If not, use every last bit of energy to make a great run into the penalty area. If you can, shoot. But if you're fouled, penalty!

TEST YOUR KNOWLEDGE

QUESTIONS

1. Who was Stevie's Liverpool hero?

2. How old was Stevie when he joined the Liverpool academy?

3. Who were Stevie's two best friends in the Liverpool youth team?

4. Stevie got into Lilleshall, the national football school – true or false?

5. Which other Premier League clubs did Stevie visit before signing his first professional contract at Liverpool?

6. Which Liverpool midfielder gave Stevie good advice and a pair of football boots?

7. What position did Stevie play in his Liverpool first-team debut?

8. When did Stevie become the Liverpool captain?

9. Which two strikers did Stevie have great partnerships with at Liverpool?

10. How many major international tournaments did Stevie play in for England?

11. Who did Liverpool play against in Stevie's final match at Anfield?

Answers below. . . No cheating!

1. *John Barnes* 2. *93*. *Michael Owen and Jason Koumas* 4. *False –
Stevie got down to the final 24 but he didn't make the final squad. He
was devastated.* 5. *Everton and Manchester United* 6. *Jamie Redknapp*
7. *Right-back* 8. *In 2003. Stevie was only 23!* 9. *Fernando Torres and
Luis Suárez* 10. *Seven – Euro 2000, 2002 World Cup, Euro 2004, 2006
World Cup, 2010 World Cup, Euro 2012, 2014 World Cup* 11. *Crystal
Palace*

HAVE YOU GOT THEM ALL?

ULTIMATE FOOTBALL HEROES